LE FRANÇAIS ESSENTIEL 1

Fundamentals of French

Gail Stein

Foreign Language Department
New York City Schools

AMSCO SCHOOL PUBLICATIONS, INC.
315 Hudson Street / New York, N.Y. 10013

Text and Cover Design by A Good Thing, Inc.
Illustrations by Felipe Galindo

Please visit our Web site at:
www.amscopub.com

When ordering this book, please specify *either* **R 774 W** *or*
LE FRANÇAIS ESSENTIEL 1: FUNDAMENTALS OF FRENCH

ISBN   1-56765-324-3

NYC Item   56765-324-2

1 2 3 4 5 6 7 8 9 10   10 09 08 07 06 05 04

Preface

Le Français essentiel 1 is designed to give students a comprehensive review and thorough understanding of the elements of the French language covered in a typical first-year course. Abundant and varied exercises conforming to the modern-day communicative approach to second language acquisition will help students master each phase of the work. Le Français essential 1 is intended as a supplementary review that provides additional practice to exercises contained in a basal textbook series.

ORGANIZATION

Le Français essentiel 1 contains 20 chapters organized around related grammatical topics. Explanations are clear, concise, and to the point. They are followed by examples demonstrating how to effectively manipulate structural elements in order to acquire natural and authentic communication skills. Practice exercises relate to daily life situations and make use of the topical vocabulary needed on this level.

GRAMMAR

Each chapter deals fully with one major grammatical topic or several closely related ones. Explanations of structures are brief and straightforward. All structural points are illustrated by several examples, in which key elements are typographically highlighted.

Le Français essentiel 1 covers a basic grammatical sequence for this level. Care has been taken to avoid the use of complex, grammatical elements. To enable the students to focus on structural practice, the vocabulary has been carefully controlled and systematically recycled throughout the book.

EXERCISES

For maximum learning efficiency, the exercises directly follow the points of grammar and their accompanying examples. They then proceed from simple integration to more challenging management of the structures presented. The exercises are set in real-life, communicative situations and require the students to perform tasks that would be expected in a variety of everyday settings. Each chapter contains activities that are personalized to stimulate student response and cooperative learning and activities to practice functional writing skills on this advanced level.

FLEXIBILITY

The integrated completeness of each chapter around a specific structural topic allows the teacher to follow any sequence suitable to the objectives of the course and the needs of the students. This flexibility is facilitated by the detailed table of contents in the front of the book.

OTHER FEATURES

The Appendix features model verb tables and the principal parts of common irregular verbs, common reflexive verbs, prepositions, and basic rules of French punctuation and syllabication. French-English and English-French vocabularies, complete the book.

Le Français essentiel 1 is an up-to-date review book that provides comprehensive coverage of the elements of level-two French. It provides clear and succinct explanations, ample practice materials, and functional, high-frequency vocabulary that will enable students of French to strengthen their second language skills and pursue proficiency on a higher level.

Gail Stein

Contents

CHAPTER 1
Numbers, Time, and Dates

1. Cardinal Numbers

0	zéro	20	vingt	90	quatre-vingt-dix	
1	un	21	vingt et un	91	quatre-vingt-onze	
2	deux	22	vingt-deux	92	quatre-vingt-douze	
3	trois	30	trente	100	cent	
4	quatre	40	quarante	101	cent un	
5	cinq	50	cinquante	200	deux cents	
6	six	60	soixante	225	deux cent vingt-cinq	
7	sept	70	soixante-dix	1.000	mille	
8	huit	71	soixante et onze	1.001	mille un	
9	neuf	72	soixante-douze	1.100	mille cent / onze cents	
10	dix	73	soixante-treize	1.200	mille deux cents /	
11	onze	74	soixante-quatorze		douze cents	
12	douze	75	soixante-quinze	2.000	deux mille	
13	treize	76	soixante-seize	10.000	dix mille	
14	quatorze	77	soixante-dix-sept	100.000	cent mille	
15	quinze	78	soixante-dix-huit	1.000.000	un million	
16	seize	79	soixante-dix-neuf	2.000.000	deux millions	
17	dix-sept	80	quatre-vingts	one billion	un milliard	
18	dix-huit	81	quatre-vingt-un	two billion	deux milliards	
19	dix-neuf	82	quatre-vingt-deux			

NOTE: 1. The conjunction *et* (and) is used only for the numbers 21, 31, 41, 51, 61, and 71. In all other compound numbers through 99 the hyphen is used. *Un* becomes *une* before a feminine noun.

vingt *et un* **garçons**	*21 boys*
vingt *et une* **filles**	*21 girls*

2. To form 70 to 79, use *soixante* plus dix, onze, douze, etc. To form 90 to 99, use *quatre-vingt* plus dix, onze, douze, etc.

3. For *quatre-vingts* (80) and multiples of *cent* drop the *s* before another number, but not before a noun.

quatre-vingts **pages**	*80 pages*
quatre-vingt-quinze **pages**	*95 pages*
deux cents **euros**	*200 euros*
deux cent cinquante **dollars**	*250 dollars*

4. *Cent* and *mille* are not preceded by the indefinite article.

cent **dollars**	*100 dollars*
mille **personnes**	*1,000 people*

5. *Mille* does not change in the plural.

   deux *mille* livres   *2,000 books*

6. *Mille* often becomes *mil* in dates.

   Il est mort en deux *mil* deux.   *He died in 2002.*

7. *Million* and *milliard* are nouns and must be followed by *de* if another noun follows.

   un million de dollars   *a (one) million dollars*
   deux milliards d'euros   *two billion euros*

8. In numerals and decimals, where English uses periods, French uses commas and vice versa. The period marking thousands is often replaced by a space.

   3.000/3 000   trois mille   *3,000   three thousand*
   0,08   zéro virgule zéro huit   *0.08   point zero eight*
   $5,50   cinq dollars cinquante   *$5.50   five dollars and fifty cents*

9. The following expressions are used in arithmetic problems in French.

   et *plus*   **divisé par** *divided by*
   moins *minus*   **font** *equals*
   fois *multiplied by*

EXERCISE A   Les maths. Spell out in French the math problems given to your little Canadian cousin.

EXAMPLE: $7 - 6 = 1$

   Sept moins six font un.

1. $9 + 4 = 13$

   _____

2. $20 - 6 = 14$

   _____

3. $16 \div 8 = 2$

   _____

4. $5 \times 3 = 15$

   _____

EXERCISE B   La logique. Complete the number sequence problems.

1. cinq, dix, _____, vingt, vingt-cinq

2. dix, neuf, _____, sept, six

3. un, deux, quatre, sept, _____

4. douze, quinze, dix-huit, _____ , vingt-quatre

5. vingt, dix-huit, seize, _____ , douze

6. vingt-quatre, vingt, dix-sept, _____ , quatorze

| EXERCISE C | **Les vêtements.**   Write out the price in French for each article of clothing.

1. (37)   La chemise coûte _____ euros.

2. (86)   La robe coûte _____ euros.

3. (74)   Le pantalon coûte _____ euros.

4. (41)   Les tennis coûtent _____ euros.

5. (99)   Le manteau coûte _____ euros.

6. (65)   Les chaussures coûtent _____ euros.

7. (52)   L'imperméable coûte _____ euros.

8. (15)   Les chaussettes coûtent _____ euros.

| EXERCISE D | **Les titres.**   Write the number mentioned in each title of a Jules Verne novel.

1. Le tour du monde en quatre-vingts jours   _____

2. Cinq semaines en ballon   _____

3. Les cinq cents millions de la Bégum   _____

4. Vingt mille lieues sous les mers   _____

5. Un capitaine de quinze ans   _____

6. Deux ans de vacances   _____

2. Ordinal Numbers

1st	premier, première	7th	septième	20th	vingtième
2nd	deuxième or second(e)	8th	huitième	21st	vingt et unième
3rd	troisième	9th	neuvième	72nd	soixante-douzième
4th	quatrième	10th	dixième	100th	centième
5th	cinquième	11th	onzième	105th	cent cinquième
6th	sixième	12th	douzième		

NOTE: 1. Ordinal numbers are adjectives and agree in gender and number with the noun they modify. *Premier* and *second* are the only ordinal numbers to have a feminine form different from the masculine form.

> **Elle est la *première* à finir.**   *She is the first one to finish.*
> **Les *seizièmes* anniversaires**
>   **sont importants aux filles.**   *Sixteenth birthdays are important to girls.*

2. Except for *premier* and *second*, ordinal numbers are formed by adding
   –ième to the cardinal numbers. Silent *e* is dropped before *–ième.*

3. Note the *u* in *cinquième* and the *v* in *neuvième.*

4. *Second(e)* generally replaces *deuxième* in a series which does not go beyond
   two.

   son *second* fils   *his/her second son*

5. Do not replace the final vowel of *le* or *la* with an apostrophe before *huit,
   huitième, onze,* and *onzième.*

   la *huitième* année   *the eighth year*
   le *onze* juillet   *July 11th*

6. Ordinal numbers are abbreviated as follows in French:

   premier 1ᵉʳ (première 1ʳᵉ)   **troisième 3ᵉ**   **vingtième 20ᵉ**

EXERCISE E   **Ils habitent où?** Tell on which floor the family lives.

10ᵉ Germaine	6ᵉ Dumas	2ᵉ Leclerc
9ᵉ Hubert	5ᵉ Manon	1ᵉʳ Crépin
8ᵉ Laurent	4ᵉ Laforêt	rez-de-chaussée
7ᵉ Lafontaine	3ᵉ Bercy	Gardien

EXAMPLE: La famille Dumas habite au **sixième étage.**

1. La famille Laurent _____ .
2. La famille Laforêt _____ .
3. La famille Hubert _____ .
4. La famille Crépin _____ .
5. La famille Manon _____ .
6. La famille Bercy _____ .

EXERCISE F   **Les sites touristiques.** Tell in which arrondissement of Paris you can find
these tourist spots.

EXAMPLE: Le Quartier Latin (5ᵉ) Le Quartier Latin se trouve dans **le cinquième arrondissement.**

1. La Bastille (11ᵉ) _____ .

2. Montmartre (18ᵉ) _____ .

3. L'Arc de Triomphe (8ᵉ) _____ .

4. La Tour Eiffel (7ᵉ) _____ .

5. Le Panthéon (5ᵉ) _____ .

6. La Bourse (2ᵉ) _____ .

3.   Time

Quelle heure est-il?	*What time is it?*
Il est une heure.	*It is one o'clock.*
Il est une heure dix.	*It is 1:10.*
Il est une heure et quart.	*It is 1:15.*
Il est une heure vingt-cinq.	*It is 1:25.*
Il est une heure et demie.	*It is 1:30.*
Il est deux heures moins vingt-cinq.	*It is 1:35.*
Il est deux heures moins vingt.	*It is 1:40.*
Il est deux heures moins le quart.	*It is 1:45.*
Il est deux heures moins dix.	*It is 1:50.*
Il est deux heures moins cinq.	*It is 1:55.*
Il est midi.	*It is noon.*
Il est minuit.	*It is midnight.*
Il est midi (minuit) et demi.	*It is half-past twelve.*

NOTE: 1. To express time after the hour, the number of minutes is placed directly after the hour; *et* is used only with *quart* and *demi(e)*. To express time before the hour, *moins* is used.

2. *Midi* and *minuit* are masculine.

3. To express the time of day, *du matin* expresses A.M., *de l'après-midi* expresses early P.M. and *du soir* expresses late P.M.

Il est cinq heures *du matin* (*de l'après-midi*).   *It is 5 A.M. (P.M.)*

4. In public announcements such as timetables, the "official" twenty-four-hour system is commonly used, with midnight as the zero hour. The words *minuit*, *midi*, *quart*, and *demi* are not used and the number of minutes is expressed by a full number.

0h10	**zéro heure dix**	*12:10 A.M.*
10h15	**dix heures quinze**	*10:15 A.M.*
14h30	**quatorze heures trente**	*2:30 P.M.*
21h45	**vingt et une heures quarante-cinq**	*9:45 P.M.*

5. To express "at" what time, use the preposition *à*.

Le film commence *à* quelle heure?   *At what time does the movie start?*
À une heure et demie.   *At 1:30.*

6. Some common time expressions are:

à une heure (deux heures) précise(s)   *at one (two) o'clock sharp*
vers onze heures   *at about 11 o'clock*
une demi-heure   *a half hour*

EXERCISE G   **Quelle heure est-il?**   Tell what time it is.

EXAMPLE: Il est **sept heures et demie.**

1. _____

2. _____

3. _____

4. _____

5. _____

6. _____

| EXERCISE H |

À l'aéroport.   You are looking at the flight departure screen at the airport. Give information about when certain flights will leave.

DÉPARTS		
HORAIRE	**DESTINATION**	**VOL**
5.55	Strasbourg	736
6.40	Bordeaux	515
7.20	Paris	294
8.45	Nice	442
9.25	Monaco	683
10.05	Marseille	125
11.10	Cannes	372

EXAMPLE: Strasbourg Le vol numéro sept cent trente-six part **à six heures moins cinq.**

1. Monaco _____ .

2. Bordeaux _____ .

3. Cannes _____ .

4. Paris _____ .

5. Marseille _____ .

6. Nice _____ .

| EXERCISE 1 | **Au musée**. Circle the time when you could visit the collection of dolls and robots from the past at this museum. |

MUSÉE NATIONAL DE MONACO

Poupées et automates d'autrefois

Collection de Galéa

Ouvert tous les jours de

10 h à 12 h 15 et de 14 h 30 à 18 h 30

---

1. At 4:55 P.M.

2. At half past noon.

3. At 7 P.M.

4. At 2:15 P.M.

4.   Days, Months, Seasons

LES JOURS DE LA SEMAINE	LES MOIS DE L'ANNÉE	LES QUATRE SAISONS
lundi Monday	**janvier** January	**l'hiver** winter
mardi Tuesday	**février** February	**le printemps** spring
mercredi Wednesday	**mars** March	**l'été** summer
jeudi Thursday	**avril** April	**l'automne** autumn
vendredi Friday	**mai** May	
samedi Saturday	**juin** June	
dimanche Sunday	**juillet** July	
	août August	
	septembre September	
	octobre October	
	novembre November	
	décembre December	

NOTE: 1. Days, months, and seasons are all masculine and are not capitalized in French.

2. To express in which months and seasons, *en* is used, except with *printemps*.

   en mai *in May*   **en été** *in the summer*   But: **au printemps** *in the spring*

3. The definite article is used with days of the week in a plural sense. If the day mentioned is a specific day, the article is omitted.

   ***Le* vendredi je joue au basket.**   *On Friday(s) I play basketball.*
   Téléphone-moi samedi.   *Call me (on) Saturday.*

EXERCISE J | **Les fêtes.** Tell in which month each holiday is celebrated.

EXAMPLE: Noël   Noël est **en décembre.**

1. le Nouvel An   _____.
2. Pâques   _____.
3. la fête des mères   _____.
4. la fête des pères   _____.
5. la fête nationale   _____.
6. le jour de la Saint Valentin   _____.

EXERCISE K | **Les sports.** Give the season(s) in which you would participate in the sports given.

EXAMPLE: la pêche   **au printemps** et **en été**

1. le basket   _____
2. la natation   _____
3. le tennis   _____
4. le football   _____
5. le base-ball   _____
6. le cyclisme   _____

5.   Dates

Quelle est la date d'aujourd'hui?   *What is today's date?*

Quel jour (de la semaine) est-ce aujourd'hui?
Quel jour sommes-nous aujourd'hui? } *What day of the week is today?*

C'est aujourd'hui mardi, le six mai.
(Aujourd'hui) nous sommes mardi, le six mai. } *Today is Tuesday, May 6th.*

NOTE: 1. In dates, *le premier* is used for the first day of the month. For all other days, cardinal numbers are used.

C'est *le premier* (*le dix*) juin.   *It's June 1st (10th).*

2. Years are commonly expressed in hundreds, as in English. The word for one thousand in dates, if used, is often written *mil.*

Il est né en *dix-neuf cent* (*mil neuf cent*) *soixante-quatorze.*   *He was born in 1974.*

3. The date follows the sequence day, month, year.

   le 12 janvier 2003 *12.1.03*   *January 12, 2003* *1/12/03*

4. A date may be written in three ways. For example,

   mardi 15 février 1999
   le mardi 15 février 1999
   mardi, le 15 février 1999

EXERCISE L **L'histoire.** Tell when these famous French people were born and when they died.

1. Jeanne d'Arc (Jan. 6, 1412 – May 30, 1431)

   Elle est née _____ .

   Elle est morte _____ .

2. Napoléon Bonaparte (Aug. 15, 1769 – May 5, 1821)

   Il est né _____ .

   Il est mort _____ .

3. Marie Curie (Nov. 7, 1867 – July 4, 1934)

   Elle est née _____ .

   Elle est morte _____ .

4. Charles de Gaulle (Nov. 22, 1890 – Nov. 9, 1970)

   Il est né _____ .

   Il est mort _____ .

EXERCISE M **Une interview.** Interview three people in your class. Ask: *"Tu es né(e) quand?"* (When were you born?) Record the day, date, year, and time of their birth. Write the information you have received.

EXAMPLE: **Jean-Paul est né vendredi, le trois mai mil neuf cent quatre-vingt huit à minuit et quart.**

1. _____ .

2. _____ .

3. _____ .

CHAPTER 2
Subject Pronouns and the Present Tense of –er Verbs

1. Subject Pronouns

A pronoun is a word used in place of a noun. A subject pronoun is used in place of a subject noun.

SUBJECT PRONOUNS			
SINGULAR		**PLURAL**	
je (j')	*I*	**nous**	*we*
tu	*you* (familiar)	**vous**	*you* (formal singular or plural)
il	*he, it*	**ils**	*they* (masculine or masculine and feminine)
elle	*she, it*	**elles**	*they* (feminine only)
on	*one, you, we , they*		

NOTE: 1. A subject pronoun normally precedes the verb.

Elle **danse bien.**   *She dances well.*

2. The *e* of *je* is dropped when the next word begins with a vowel or vowel sound.

J'arrive.   *I'm coming.*

J'habite à Paris.   *I live in Paris.*

3. *Tu* is used to address a friend, a relative, a child, or a pet. When addressing one person, *vous* is used to show respect, or to speak to an older person or someone one does not know well. When addressing two or more persons, *vous* is always used no matter what the relationship.

Tu **es un bon ami.** (informal)

Vous **êtes un bon ami.** (formal) } *You are a good friend.*

Vous **êtes de bons amis.**   *You are good friends.*

4. *Il, elle, ils, elles,* refer to both persons and things. Use *ils* to refer to several nouns of different genders.

La fille travaille.	*The girl is working.*
Elle **travaille.**	*She is working.*
La machine fonctionne.	*The machine is working.*
Elle **fonctionne.**	*It is working.*
L'homme et la femme chantent.	*The man and the woman are singing.*
Ils **chantent.**	*They are singing.*

5. *On* means one or someone and may also refer to an indefinite you, we, they, or people in general. In spoken French, *on* often replaces *nous*.

On doit étudier pour réussir.   *You have to (One must) study to succeed.*
On va au café?   *Shall we go to the café?*

EXERCISE A   **Ma famille.** You are telling a friend about the jobs of the people in your family. Replace the name of your relatives with the appropriate pronoun.

EXAMPLE: *Mon frère* est étudiant.   **Il est étudiant.**

1. Mes grands-parents sont avocats.

    _____ .

2. Mon père est ingénieur.

    _____ .

3. Ma mère est professeur.

    _____ .

4. Mes sœurs sont infirmières.

    _____ .

5. Mes cousins sont mécaniciens.

    _____ .

6. Ma tante et mon oncle sont docteurs.

    _____ .

EXERCISE B   **Les pièces.** Your friend is asking you the location of the furniture or appliances in your house. Answer him using the appropriate pronoun instead of repeating their names.

EXAMPLE: La table de nuit?   **Elle** est dans la chambre.

1. La télévision?   _____ est dans le living.

2. Les petites étagères?   _____ sont dans le salon.

3. Le four à micro-ondes?   _____ est dans la cuisine.

4. Les grands lits?   _____ sont dans la chambre.

5. La lampe et le miroir?   _____ sont dans la chambre d'amis.

6. La table et les chaises?   _____ sont dans la salle à manger.

EXERCISE C   **Vos opinions.** You have your opinions about people. Tell them how you feel by using *tu* or *vous*.

1. Maman et papa, _____ êtes très intelligents.

2. M. Brun, _____ êtes un docteur sympathique.

3. Jean, _____ es un bon ami.

4. Fifi, _____ es un chien fidèle.

5. Mme Ronsard, _____ êtes charmante.

6. Amélie, _____ es une fille patiente.

| EXERCISE D | **Le succès.** To succeed in your French class, one must do certain things. Express what that is. |

EXAMPLE: participer à la classe.   **On doit** participer à la classe.

1. parler français tout le temps

_____ .

2. étudier beaucoup

_____ .

3. poser des questions

_____ .

4. travailler dur

_____ .

5. préparer les devoirs

_____ .

6. écouter le prof

_____ .

2.   Forms of the Present Tense in *–er* Verbs

The present tense of *–er* verbs is formed by dropping the *–er* infinitive ending and adding the ending highlighted below.

danser *to dance*		
SINGULAR	je **danse**	*I dance, I am dancing*
	tu **danses**	*you dance, you are dancing*
	il **danse**	*he dances, he is dancing*
	elle **danse**	*she dances, she is dancing*
	on **danse**	*one dances, one is dancing*
PLURAL	nous **dansons**	*we dance, we are dancing*
	vous **dansez**	*you dance, you are dancing*
	ils **dansent**	*they dance, they are dancing*
	elles **dansent**	*they dance, they are dancing*

Common –*er* Verbs:

accompagner *to accompany*	**inviter** *to invite*
aider *to help*	**jouer** *to play*
aimer *to like, love*	**laver** *to wash*
apporter *to bring*	**marcher** *to walk*
arriver *to arrive*	**monter** *to go up*
bavarder *to chat*	**organiser** *to organize*
chanter *to sing*	**oublier** *to forget*
chercher *to look for*	**parler** *to speak*
compter *to count*	**participer** *to participate*
continuer *to continue*	**passer** *to pass, spend* (*time*)
coûter *to cost*	**penser** *to think*
crier *to shout*	**porter** *to wear, carry*
cuisiner *to cook*	**préparer** *to prepare*
déjeuner *to eat lunch*	**présenter** *to present, introduce*
demander *to ask*	**prêter** *to lend*
dépenser *to spend* (*money*)	**quitter** *to leave, remove*
dîner *to dine*	**rater** *to fail*
donner *to give*	**regarder** *to look at, watch*
écouter *to listen* (*to*)	**rencontrer** *to meet*
emprunter *to borrow*	**rentrer** *to return*
entrer *to enter*	**réparer** *to repair*
étudier *to study*	**rester** *to remain, stay*
expliquer *to explain*	**téléphoner** *to telephone*
fermer *to close*	**travailler** *to work*
gagner *to win, earn*	**trouver** *to find*
garder *to keep, watch, take care of*	**utiliser** *to use*
habiter *to live* (*in*)	

3.   Uses of the Present Tense

A verb expresses an action or a state of being and is generally shown in its "to" form, also called the infinitive. Verbs are used in the present tense as follows:

(1) To express what is happening or what does happen now.

> **Je travaille.**   *I work. I'm working. I do work.*

(2) To imply the immediate future.

> **Il arrive ce soir.**   *He's arriving this evening.*

NOTE: When one subject is followed by two verbs, the first verb is conjugated and the second verb remains in the infinitive.

Elle aime danser.   *She likes to dance.*

EXERCISE E   **En classe.** Express what different people do in different classes.

EXAMPLE: (jouer) Dans la classe de musique la fille _____ du piano.
Dans la classe de musique la fille **joue** du piano.

1. (compter)   Dans la classe de maths je _____ .

2. (parler)   Dans la classe de français nous _____ .

3. (cuisiner)   Dans la classe d'art culinaire les garçons _____ .

4. (chanter)   Dans la classe de musique vous _____ .

5. (dessiner)   Dans la classe d'art elles _____ .

6. (jouer)   Dans la classe de gymnastique tu _____ à tous les sports.

7. (utiliser)   Dans la classe d'informatique il _____ un ordinateur.

8. (penser)   Dans la classe d'histoire elle _____ au passé.

EXERCISE F   **Ce soir.** Write what these people will be doing this evening.

EXAMPLE: il/bavarder avec son ami.   Il **bavarde** avec son ami.

1. je/téléphoner à mes copains

_____ .

2. vous/dîner au restaurant

_____ .

3. elles/marcher en ville

_____ .

4. nous/regarder la télévision

_____ .

5. on/écouter des disques

_____ .

6. elle/jouer avec l'ordinateur

_____ .

7. ils/organiser une boum

_____ .

8. tu/rester à la maison

_____ .

EXERCISE G   **Le dîner.**   Talk about dinner at this girl's house by filling in the blanks with the correct form of the verb. Use the vocabulary provided.

aider	cuisiner	préparer
apporter	dîner	rentrer
commencer	inviter	
couper	laver	

Dans ma famille nous —————— 1. à sept heures du soir. Quand nous —————— 2.

à la maison vers six heures ma mère —————— 3. tout de suite à préparer le dîner. Papa et

moi, nous —————— 4. toujours maman. Papa, lui, il —————— 5. les légumes sous

l'eau froide et moi je les —————— 6. en petits morceaux. Nous —————— 7.

toujours une salade magnifique. Maman —————— 8. le reste. Quelquefois mes parents

—————— 9. des amis à dîner avec nous. Nos invités —————— 10. des fleurs ou

un dessert. Notre dîner est toujours formidable.

EXERCISE H   **Après les devoirs.**   Take turns with a friend expressing what you do after you've finished your homework. Consider four different activities.

———————————————————————————————

———————————————————————————————

———————————————————————————————

———————————————————————————————

EXERCISE I   Write a note in French to your pen pal telling what your hobbies are.

———————————————————————————————

———————————————————————————————

———————————————————————————————

———————————————————————————————

———————————————————————————————

———————————————————————————————

CHAPTER 3
The Present Tense of *-ir* Verbs

The present tense of regular *-ir* verbs is formed by dropping the infinitive ending (*-ir*) and adding the endings highlighted below.

		choisir	*to choose*
SINGULAR	je	chois*is*	*I choose, I am choosing*
	tu	chois*is*	*you choose, you are choosing*
	il	chois*it*	*he chooses, he is choosing*
	elle	chois*it*	*she chooses, she is choosing*
	on	chois*it*	*one chooses, one is choosing*
PLURAL	nous	chois*issons*	*we choose, we are choosing*
	vous	chois*issez*	*you choose, you are choosing*
	ils	chois*issent*	*they choose, they are choosing*
	elles	chois*issent*	*they choose, they are choosing*

Common *-ir* Verbs

applaudir *to applaud, clap*
bâtir *to build*
désobéir *to disobey*
finir *to finish*
grandir *to grow*
grossir *to become fat*
guérir *to cure*
maigrir *to become thin*

obéir *to obey*
punir *to punish*
réfléchir *to reflect, think*
remplir *to fill* (out)
réussir *to succeed*
rôtir *to roast*
rougir *to blush*
saisir *to seize*

EXERCISE A **Le lecture.** Express what each person finishes reading by using the correct form of the verb *finir*.

1. Je _____ la revue.

2. Vous _____ le magazine.

3. Il _____ le poème.

4. Nous _____ le livre.

5. Tu _____ le journal.

6. Elles _____ le conte.

7. Elle _____ l'article.

8. Ils _____ la pièce.

9. On _____ l'histoire.

| EXERCISE B | **Le travail.** Match the person with the service he performs. Then write a complete sentence. |

EXAMPLE: Un directeur ____   applaudir les acteurs

Un directeur **applaudit les acteurs.**

1. Un ingénieur ____

_____

2. Un juge ____

_____

3. Un docteur ____

_____

4. Un chef ____

_____

5. Un secrétaire ____

_____

6. Un étudiant ____

_____

a. réussir à l'école.
b. bâtir les maisons
c. rôtir la viande
d. punir les criminels
e. remplir les formulaires
f. guérir les malades

| EXERCISE C | **À la fête.** Express what is happening at the party by giving the correct form of the verb. |

EXAMPLE: Jean/obéir aux règles.   Jean **obéit** aux règles.

1. tu/réussir à danser

_____

2. Suzanne/remplir les verres de soda

_____

3. vous/saisir l'occasion de parler à tout le monde

_____

4. les filles/rougir quand elles dansent

_____

5. nous/finir par nous amuser

_____

6. on/rôtir un poulet

_____

7. je/grossir, c'est sûr

_____

8. les garçons/réfléchir avant de parler

_____

EXERCISE D **Des situations différentes.** Write what happens to each person in the situations they encounter. Use the vocabulary provided.

| désobéir | maigrir | réussir |
| grossir | obéir | rougir |

EXAMPLE: Quand elles arrivent à la maison elles **finissent** leurs devoirs.

1. Quand il mange beaucoup de chocolats il _____ .

2. Quand tu fais tous les devoirs et tu travailles sérieusement tu _____ .

3. Quand nous n'écoutons pas les règles nous _____ .

4. Quand elle est embarassée elle _____ .

5. Quand vous mangez très peu vous _____ .

6. Quand ils écoutent leurs parents ils _____ .

EXERCISE E Work with a partner. Discuss and then write a list of eight activities that complete this phrase:

Je réussis quand . . .

EXAMPLE: j'étudie beaucoup.

1. _____ .
2. _____ .
3. _____ .
4. _____ .
5. _____ .
6. _____ .
7. _____ .
8. _____ .

EXERCISE F   **La carte.**   You are in a French restaurant with a friend. Read the menu and then answer your friend's questions in a complete sentence.

L'Auberge Gourmande

Entrées

Œufs mayonnaise 24	Assiette de crudités 30
Salade d'épinards 28	Caviar d'aubergines 32

Saumon mariné 40

Soupes

Consommé de poulet 20	Vichyssoise 32
Bouillon d'écrevisses 24	Soupe à l'oignon 46

Bisque de homard 56

Plats

Saucisson chaud 62	Selle d'agneau 78
Poulet rôti 68	Médaillons de veau 86
Tartare de saumon 72	Filet de bœuf 102

Légumes

Frites 12	Riz 14
Pâtes. 12	Gratin de macaronis 16

Haricots verts 20

Desserts

Tarte aux pommes 32	Profiteroles au chocolat 36
Crème brûlée 32	Gâteau au chocolat 38

Crêpes Suzette 38

1.   Qu'est-ce que tu choisis comme entrée?   _____

2.   Qu'est-ce que tu choisis comme soupe?   _____

3. Qu'est-ce que tu choisis comme plat principal? _____

4. Qu'est-ce que tu choisis comme légumes? _____

5. Qu'est-ce que tu choisis comme dessert? _____

EXERCISE G   **Les résolutions.**   Your last New Year's resolution was to lose a little weight. Write a note in French telling a friend how one can accomplish this goal.

_____

_____

_____

_____

_____

_____

_____

_____

_____

_____

_____

CHAPTER 4
The Present Tense of *–re* Verbs

The present tense of *–re* verbs is formed by dropping the infinitive ending (*-re*) and adding the highlighted endings below.

perdre *to lose*			
SINGULAR	je	perd**s**	*I lose, I am losing*
	tu	perd**s**	*you lose, you are losing*
	il	perd	*he loses, he is losing*
	elle	perd	*she loses, she is losing*
	on	perd	*one loses, one is losing*
PLURAL	nous	perd**ons**	*we lose, we are losing*
	vous	perd**ez**	*you lose, you are losing*
	ils	perd**ent**	*they lose, they are losing*
	elles	perd**ent**	*they lose, they are losing*

Common *–re* verbs:

attendre *to wait (for)*   **entendre** *to hear*

correspondre *to correspond*   **rendre** *to return*

défendre *to defend*   **répondre (à)** *to answer*

descendre *to go down*   **vendre** *to sell*

EXERCISE A **Les professions.** Match the person with what he does and conjugate the verb to form a complete sentence.

EXAMPLE: Un conducteur de bus ____   attendre des passagers

Un conducteur de bus **attend des passagers.**

1. Un vendeur ____

   _____

2. Un chef d'orchestre ____

   _____

3. Un soldat ____

   _____

4. Un homme d'affaires ____

   _____

5. Un professeur ____

   _____

6. Un réceptionniste ____

   _____

a. défendre son pays
b. répondre au téléphone
c. correspondre avec ses clients
d. vendre de la marchandise
e. entendre de la musique
f. rendre les examens aux élèves

EXERCISE B   **Les transports.** These people are all in a hurry to get to work, but unfortunately they have to wait. Express what they are waiting for by using the correct form of the verb *attendre.*

EXAMPLE: il/le tramway   Il **attend** le tramway.

1. je/le bus   _____

2. elle/le train   _____

3. nous/le métro   _____

4. tu/un taxi   _____

5. vous/l'autocar   _____

6. ils/la voiture de leur ami   _____

EXERCISE C   **Après l'école.** Express what your classmates and you do after school.

1. (descendre)   Je _____ en ville.

2. (correspondre) Richard _____ avec ses amis.

3. (rendre)   Lucie et Douglas _____ des livres à la bibliothèque.

4. (répondre)   On _____ au téléphone.

5. (vendre)   Tu _____ des glaces sur la plage.

6. (attendre)   Alice _____ ses amies.

7. (défendre)   Josette et Lucien _____ leurs amis.

8. (perdre)   Vous _____ patience.

EXERCISE D   **Chez le disquaire.** Complete the story about two boys in a record store by using the following verbs and conjugating them.

attendre	entendre	répondre
défendre	perdre	vendre
descendre	rendre	

Alain _____ son ami, Bernard, à la sortie de l'école. Les deux garçons
              1.

_____ en ville. Ils entrent dans un magasin qui _____ des CD. Dans le
        2.   3.

magasin ils _____ de la musique. Alain est là parce qu'il _____ un CD
                4.   5.

défectueux. Malheureusement, le vendeur est très occupé parce qu'il _____ aux
                                                                              6.

questions d'un autre client. Il ignore les deux garçons. Alors, Alain _____
                                                                              7.

patience. Bernard et lui _____ l'escalier du magasin pour regarder des cassettes
                              8.

en bas.   Après dix minutes le vendeur ——————— chercher les deux garçons.
9.

Il ——————— son retard et il ——————— l'histoire du CD défectueux. Il ———————,
10.   11.   12.

"Nous ——————— ce CD. Si tu ——————— je ——————— ton argent avec plaisir."
13.   14.   15.

EXERCISE E   Work with a partner.   Take turns asking each other about stores in France.
Follow the example:

YOU: On vend quoi dans une boucherie?

PARTNER: On vend de la viande. On vend quoi dans une pâtisserie?

Use these stores: un magasin de disques, un supermarché, une boulangerie, une pharmacie,
une parfumerie, une boutique, une fruiterie.

EXERCISE F   **Vos activités.**   Write a note in French to a friend giving information about
yourself. Use the following verbs:

attendre   défendre   rendre
correspondre   perdre   répondre

_____

_____

_____

_____

_____

_____

_____

_____

CHAPTER 5
Negation

1. Negative Constructions

In a negative construction, *ne* precedes the verb and *pas* follows it. *Ne* becomes *n'* before a vowel or a vowel sound (*h* or *y*).

Je *ne* regarde *pas* la télé.	*I'm not watching television.*
Elle *ne* rougit *pas*.	*She isn't blushing.*
Nous *n'*entendons *pas* la musique.	*We don't hear the music.*
Ils *n'*habitent *pas* cette maison.	*They don't live in that house.*

EXERCISE A **La paresse.** It's Sunday and everyone is lazy. Express the chores that the people aren't doing.

EXAMPLE: Paul/passer l'aspirateur   Il **ne passe pas** l'aspirateur.

1. tu/répondre au téléphone   _____

2. vous/cuisiner   _____

3. Louise/ranger le salon   _____

4. les garçons/vider les ordures   _____

5. je/rôtir le porc   _____

6. les filles/ descendre en ville   _____

7. on/correspondre avec des amis   _____

8. Jacques/finir ses devoirs   _____

2. Other Negative Forms

a. The other most common negative forms are:

ne...jamais	*never*
ne...personne	*no one, nobody, anyone, anybody*
ne...plus	*no longer, anymore*
ne...rien	*nothing, anything*

b. Position of negatives

Ne comes before the conjugated verb and the other part of the negative comes after the conjugated verb. Note that, where applicable, *personne* follows the infinitive.

Il *ne* danse *jamais*.	*He never dances.*
Je *n'*entends *personne*.	*I don't hear anybody.*

> **Je** *n'***entends parler** *personne.*   *I don't hear anybody speaking.*
> **Ils** *ne* **travaillent** *plus.*   *They aren't working any more.*
> **Tu** *ne* **finis** *rien.*   *You don't finish anything.*

EXERCICE B   **La vieillesse.** Grandpa Jacques is 88 years old. Express what he no longer does.

EXAMPLE: marcher vite   Il **ne** marche **plus** vite.

1. grossir _____

2. descendre en ville _____

3. travailler _____

4. perdre patience _____

5. désobéir à son docteur _____

6. manger après 7 h. _____

EXERCICE C   **La négativité.** For the people below, the answer is "nothing." Answer the questions about them using *rien*.

EXAMPLE: Tu saisis quelque chose?   Tu **ne** saisis **rien.**

1. Tu cherches quelque chose? _____

2. Il descend quelque chose de son placard? _____

3. Nous finissons quelque chose d'important? _____

4. Vous aimez quelque chose? _____

5. J'oublie quelque chose? _____

6. Elles applaudissent quelque chose? _____

EXERCICE D   **Le tempérament.** Some people are very mild-mannered and have even temperaments. Express what they never do.

EXAMPLE: travailler vite   Ils **ne travaillent jamais** vite.

1. perdre courage _____

2. désobeir _____

3. critiquer leurs amis _____

4. crier _____

5. répondre avec impatience _____

6. choisir de pleurer _____

EXERCISE E   **Personne.**   It's been a rough day. Say that the subject wants nothing to do with anybody.

EXAMPLE: il/écouter   Il **n'écoute personne.**

1. je/défendre   _____

2. nous/attendre   _____

3. vous/embrasser   _____

4. Claudine/aimer   _____

5. tu/rencontrer   _____

6. ils/regarder   _____

   c. *Rien* and *personne* may be used as subjects, preceding the verb; *ne* remains before the conjugated verb.

     ***Rien n'*est certain.**   *Nothing is certain.*
     ***Personne ne* vient.**   *Nobody is coming*

EXERCISE F   **L'optimisme.**   Show your optimism by expressing that nothing gets in your way.

EXAMPLE: difficile   **Rien n'**est difficile.

1. horrible   _____

2. terrible   _____

3. mauvais   _____

4. impossible   _____

5. inutile   _____

6. désastreux   _____

EXERCISE G   **Un prof sévère.**   Express what no one does in M. Deneuve's French class.

EXAMPLE: oublier son livre   **Personne n'**oublie son livre.

1. finir ses devoirs en classe   _____

2. désobéir au prof   _____

3. répondre à voix basse   _____

4. parler en anglais   _____

5. crier à haute voix   _____

6. manger en classe   _____

d. The second part of a negative may be used alone, except for *pas* and *plus* which require an adjective or an adverb.

Qui parle?	*Who is speaking?*
Personne.	*No one.*
Qu'est-ce que tu cherches?	*What are you looking for?*
Rien.	*Nothing.*
Tu rates tes cours?	*Do you fail your courses?*
Jamais.	*Never.*
Tu joues au golf?	*Do you play golf?*
Pas souvent.	*Not often.*

e. *Jamais* used in the construction *ne...jamais* or by itself means never. *Jamais* in a clause without *ne* sometimes means ever.

Il *ne* reste *jamais* après les classes.	*He never stays after school.*
Jamais?	*Never?*
Restes-tu *jamais* après les classes?	*Do you ever stay after school?*
Non, jamais.	*No, never.*

EXERCISE H   **Une courte réponse.**   Answer these questions about your eating habits in the negative with just one or two words.

1. Qu'est-ce que tu manges de sucré?   _____

2. Tu aimes beaucoup la viande?   _____

3. Tu manges souvent du poisson?   _____

4. Qui te conseille de suivre un régime?   _____

3.   Common Negative Expressions

ça ne fait rien   *It doesn't matter.*

Il ne finit pas le travail.	*He isn't finishing the work.*
Ça ne fait rien.	*It doesn't matter.*

de rien/il n'y a pas de quoi.   *You're welcome*

Merci beaucoup.	*Thank you very much.*
De rien. (Il n'y a pas de quoi.)	*You're welcome.*

jamais de la vie!   *Never! Out of the question! not on your life!*

Tu fumes?	*Do you smoke?*
Jamais de la vie!	*Never!*

pas du tout   *not at all*
Tu aimes ce film?   *Do you like this movie?*
Pas du tout.   *Not at all.*

pas encore   *not yet*
Il vient?   *Is he coming?*
Pas encore.   *Not yet.*

pas maintentant   *not now*
Il quitte la maison?   *Is he leaving the house?*
Pas maintenant.   *Not now.*

pas aujourd'hui   *not today*
Tu travailles?   *Are you working?*
Pas aujourd'hui.   *Not today.*

EXERCISE 1   **Une réponse honnête.**   Express how you would answer a friend in the following situations.

1. Tu acceptes une invitation à dîner chez Jean, mais une fois arrivé, tu ne manges pas le repas.

   Il te demande pourquoi. Tu réponds: _____ mais je n'aime pas le poulet.

2. Tu vas au cinéma avec ton ami. Vous regardez une histoire d'amour ridicule. Ton ami

   demande si tu aimes le film. Tu réponds: _____ .

3. Tom ami désire monter à motocyclette. C'est très dangereux. Ton ami insiste que tu montes.

   Tu réponds: _____ .

4. Ta mère désire que tu ranges ta chambre. Tu préfères regarder la télé. Elle demande si ta

   chambre est propre. Tu réponds: _____ .

5. Ton ami désire aller à la plage aujourd'hui. Il fait très chaud et tu es malade. Ton ami te

   téléphone pour t'inviter à la plage. Tu réponds: _____ .

6. Tu donnes un joli cadeau à ton ami pour fêter son anniversaire. C'est un cadeau parfait.

   Ton ami dit, "merci." Tu réponds: _____ .

EXERCISE J   Work with a partner. Tell each other four things you don't do when you
have a lot of homework to finish.

_____

_____

_____

_____

EXERCISE K   Your friend invited you to go to an after-school club. Write a note explaining
why you can't go.

_____

_____

_____

_____

_____

_____

_____

_____

_____

_____

_____

CHAPTER 6
Interrogation

1. Using Intonation

In spoken French nowadays, an interrogative intonation (shown in writing by a question mark) is often all that is needed to change a statement into a question. This is especially the case for questions to be answered by yes or no.

Nous bavardons trop?	*Do we chat too much?*
Oui, **beaucoup trop.**	*Yes, much too much.*

2. Using *Est-ce que*

A question may also be formed by beginning a statement with *est-ce que,* which becomes *est-ce qu'* before a vowel or silent *h*.

Est-ce que **nous bavardons trop?**	*Do we chat too much?*
*Est-ce qu'***Henri lave la voiture?**	*Is Henry washing the car?*

3. Using *N'est-ce pas*

A question may also be formed by ending a statement with the tag *n'est-ce pas,* isn't that so? right? isn't (doesn't) he/she? aren't (don't) they/we/you?

Nous bavardons trop, *n'est-ce pas?*	*We chat too much, don't we (right?)*

EXERCISE A   **Un garçon sportif.** Ask Thierry if he does the following. Use intonation, *est-ce que,* and *n'est-ce pas.*

EXAMPLE: regarder les matches à la télé   Tu regardes les matches à la télé**?**

Est-ce que tu regardes les matches à la télé?

Tu regardes les matches à la télé, **n'est-ce pas?**

1. aimer les sports   _____

_____

_____

2. collectionner les cartes de base-ball   _____

_____

_____

3. jouer au foot   _____

_____

_____

4. applaudir les joueurs excellents   _____

    _____

    _____

5. gagner beaucoup de matches de basket   _____

    _____

    _____

6. perdre beaucoup de matches de volley   _____

    _____

    _____

| **EXERCISE B** | **Les opinions.**   Ask about people in three ways. Use intonation, *est-ce que* and *n'est-ce pas?*. |

EXAMPLE: Il est sociable.   Il est sociable**?**
                                       Est-ce qu'il est sociable?
                                       Il est sociable, **n'est-ce pas**?

1. Elle est dynamique.   _____

    _____

    _____

2. Ils sont optimistes.   _____

    _____

    _____

3. Ils sont aimables.   _____

    _____

    _____

4. Nous sommes sympathiques.   _____

    _____

    _____

5. Vous êtes populaire.   _____

    _____

    _____

6. Tu es honnête.   _____

    _____

    _____

4.   Using Inversion

A question may also be formed by reversing the order of the subject pronoun and the conjugated verb and joining them with a hyphen.

Nous bavardons trop.	*Bavardons-nous* **trop?**
Tu parles français.	*Parles-tu* **français?**

NOTE: 1. This construction is less frequent in spoken French and almost never occurs in the first person singular *(je)*.

2. With *il, elle,* or *on* and a verb form ending in a vowel (usually an *–er* verb), *-t-* is added between the verb and the pronoun to separate the vowels.

Il aime les sports.	*Aime-t-il* **les sports?**
Elle étudie beaucoup.	*Étudie-t-elle* **beaucoup?**
On cherche le cinéma.	*Cherche-t-on* **le cinéma?**

EXERCISE C   **La boum.** Ask what Antoinette is doing to prepare for her party. Use inversion.

EXAMPLE: Elle demande la permission à ses parents.

           Demande-t-elle la permission à ses parents?

1. Elle invite tous ses amis. _____

2. Elle range la maison. _____

3. Elle descend les décorations. _____

4. Elle prépare un gâteau. _____

5. Elle choisit les CD de rock. _____

6. Elle finit les préparatifs. _____

7. Elle attend les suggestions de ses amis. _____

8. Elle répond aux questions de ses parents. _____

EXERCISE D   **En vacances.** Ask what sports these people play while on vacation. Use inversion.

EXAMPLE: ils/plonger   **Plongent-ils?**

1. tu/skier _____

2. on/patiner _____

3. vous/nager _____

4. nous/chasser _____

5. elles/marcher _____

6. il/jouer au volley _____

5. Negative Questions

A negative question can be formed using intonation.

Tu n'aimes pas la mousse au chocolat?   *Don't you like chocolate mousse?*
Le chien n'obéit pas?   *Doesn't the dog obey?*

A negative question can also be formed using *est-ce que*.

Est-ce que je ne parle pas bien?   *Don't I speak well?*

NOTE: The word *si* is used to give an affirmative response to a negative question.

     Est-ce qu'il ne danse pas bien?   *Doesn't he dance well?*
     Si, il danse très bien.   *Yes, he dances very well.*

EXERCISE E   **Au théâtre.** You are at a play. Ask negative questions about what people are doing there and what they observe. Use intonation and *est-ce que*.

EXAMPLE: la chanteuse/chanter bien
     La chanteuse ne chante pas bien?
     Est-ce que la chanteuse ne chante pas bien?

1. l'acteur principal/joue bien son rôle

2. les acteurs/rendre le public heureux

3. je/applaudir assez

4. vous/réussir à comprendre l'histoire

5. tu/apprécier la musique

6. nous/parler à voix basse

6.   Interrogative Adverbs

Interrogative adverbs can be used to form questions seeking information by using intonation, *est-ce que,* and inversion. The most common interrogative adverbs are:

combien?	*how much, many?*	**d'où**	*from where?*
comment?	*how?*	**pourquoi?**	*why?*
où	*where*	**quand?**	*when*

a. In colloquial, spoken French, questions are often formed by placing the interrogative adverb after the verb (except *pourquoi*):

> **Tu es *d'où*?**   *Where are you from?*
>
> **Cette robe coûte *combien*?**   *How much does this dress cost?*

b. Questions beginning with an interrogative adverb are frequently formed by placing *est-ce que* after the adverb:

> **Pourquoi *est-ce qu*'elle pleure?**   *Why is she crying?*
>
> **Comment *est-ce qu*'il répond?**   *How does he answer?*

c. A question beginning with an interrogative adverb can also be formed by placing the inverted verb and subject pronoun after the adverb:

> **Quand *rentrent-ils*?**   *When are they returning?*
>
> **Où *habitez-vous*?**   *Where do you live?*

> **NOTE:** With *combien, comment, où, d'où,* and *quand,* when the subject is a noun, and the verb has no object, a question may be formed by inverting the order of the subject and the verb.
>
> > **Combien *coûte cette robe*?**   *How much does this dress cost?*
> >
> > **Comment *s'appelle ce garçon*?**   *What's that boy's name?*

EXERCISE F   **Au magasin.** You are shopping in a large department store in Canada. Use intonation, *est-ce que,* and inversion when asking the salesperson about the form of payment.

EXAMPLE: pourquoi en dollars   Pourquoi on paye en dollars?
                                    Pourquoi est-ce qu'on paye en dollars?
                                    Pourquoi paye-t-on en dollars?

1. quand? _____

   _____

   _____

2. combien? _____

   _____

   _____

3. où   _____

_____

_____

4. comment?   _____

_____

_____

EXERCISE G   **Un correspondant.**   You pen pal is visiting from France. Write questions using intonation, *est-ce que* and inversion that would give the information provided.

EXAMPLE: Il arrive <u>de France</u>.   Il arrive **d'où?**
                                              D'où **est-ce qu'**il arrive?
                                              D'où **arrive-t-il**?

1. Il paye son billet <u>cinq cents dollars</u>.   _____

_____

_____

2. Il arrive <u>le vingt-deux juillet</u>.   _____

_____

_____

3. Il est <u>de Nice</u>.   _____

_____

_____

4. Il arrive <u>à l'aéroport O'Hare</u>.   _____

_____

_____

5. Il visite Chicago <u>pour pratiquer l'anglais</u>.   _____

_____

_____

6. Il est <u>grand et blond</u>.   _____

_____

_____

EXERCISE H   **Les passagers.** Ask questions about the passengers traveling in your train compartment.

EXAMPLE: ce monsieur/habiter où   Où **habite ce monsieur?**

1. cette fille/arriver d'où   _____

2. ces dames/payer combien   _____

3. ce garçon/descendre où   _____

4. ces hommes/travailler comment   _____

5. ces enfants/obéir quand   _____

7.   Interrogative Adjectives

The interrogative adjective *quel* (which? what?) agrees with the noun it modifies and may be used with intonation, *est-ce que,* and inversion.

	MASCULINE	FEMININE
SINGULAR	quel	quelle
PLURAL	quels	quelles

Tu aimes quelle chanson?
Quelle chanson *est-ce que* **tu aimes?**   } *What song do you like?*
Quelle chanson *aimes-tu?*

NOTE: 1. The only verb that may follow *quel* directly is *être* (to be).

Quel est **ton numéro de téléphone?**   *What's your phone number?*

2. *Quel* may be preceded by a preposition.

Elle parle *de quel* **film?**   *What movie is she speaking about?*
Pour quel **magasin est-ce que**
  tu travailles?   *For which store do you work?*
À quelle **heure arrive-t-il?**   *At what time is he arriving?*

3. The forms of *quel* are used in exclamations to express what a...! or what...!

Quelle **grande maison!**   *What a big house!*
Quelles **histoires comiques!**   *What funny stories!*

EXERCISE I   **Les renseignements.** You are asking for directions to see tourist attractions that interest you. The person you ask needs more information.

EXAMPLE: Je cherche une église.   — **Quelle** église?

1. Je cherche un musée. _____

2. Je cherche des monuments. _____

3. Je cherche une cathédrale. _____

4. Je cherche des boutiques. _____

EXERCISE J   **La lecture.** Give your opinion of the things you've read by using an exclamation.

EXAMPLE: Ces articles sont ennuyeux.   **Quels** articles ennuyeux!

1. Cette histoire est comique.   _____

2. Ce film est ridicule.   _____

3. Ces livres sont intéressants.   _____

4. Ce conte est absurde.   _____

5. Ces pièces sont dramatiques.   _____

6. Ces poèmes sont splendides.   _____

8.   Interrogative Pronouns

	SUBJECT	DIRECT OBJECT
PEOPLE	**qui?** *who?*	**qui?** *whom?*
THINGS	**qu'est-ce qui** *what?*	**que?** *what?*

NOTE: The *e* of *que* is dropped before a word beginning with a vowel; the *i* of *qui* is never dropped.

a. Interrogative Pronouns as Subjects

Qui? (who?) is used for people. *Qu'est-ce qui?* (what?) is used for things. As subjects they are followed immediately by a verb in the third person singular (*il* form).

Qui parle?   *Who is speaking?*
Qu'est-ce qui arrive?   *What's happening?*

EXERCISE K   **En classe.**   Write questions about what happens in class using *qui* or *qu'est-ce qui.*

EXEMPLES: Un élève crie.   **Qui** crie?
                    Le téléphone sonne.   **Qu'est-ce qui** sonne?

1. Le livre tombe.   _____

2. Le directeur arrive.   _____

3. <u>La cloche</u> sonne. _____

4. <u>Une note</u> arrive. _____

5. <u>Un élève</u> tombe. _____

6. <u>Un parent</u> téléphone. _____

b. Interrogative Pronouns as Direct Objects

Qui and *que* can be used with intonation, with *est-ce que* or with inversion.

Tu admires *qui?*
***Qui est-ce que* tu admires?** } *Whom do you admire?*
***Qui* admires-tu?**

***Qu'est-ce que* tu admires?** } *What do you admire?*
***Qu'*admires-tu?**

NOTE: 1. *Qui* can be preceded by a preposition.

***De (À) qui* parles-tu?**   *About (To) whom are you speaking?*

2. *Que* becomes *quoi* when used at the end of question with intonation.

Tu admires *quoi?*   *What do you admire?*

EXERCISE L **Les opinions.** Write the questions your friend asked you about your opinion using *qui* or *que*. Base the questions on the answers provided. Write each question in three ways.

EXAMPLE: J'admire mon professeur de français.   Tu admires **qui?**
                                                 Qui est-ce que tu admires?
                                                 Qui admires-tu?

1. Je défends mes idées. _____

_____

_____

2. Je respecte mes parents. _____

_____

_____

3. J'aime ma liberté. _____

_____

_____

4. Je déteste la guerre.   _____

_____

_____

5. Je conseille mes amis.   _____

_____

_____

6. J'écoute mon meilleur ami.   _____

_____

_____

EXERCISE M   Work with a partner.   Taking turns ask and write four questions about your family and friends.

_____

_____

_____

_____

_____

_____

_____

EXERCISE N   **Un message électronique.**   You have a new pen pal, Claudine.   Write her an e-mail where you ask her whatever you'd like to know.

_____

_____

_____

_____

_____

_____

_____

_____

CHAPTER 7
Spelling Changes in Certain Verbs

1. -cer Verbs

In the present tense, verbs ending in -cer change c to ç before o to retain the soft c sound. Thus, the first person plural form of the present tense ends in -çons.

placer *to place*			
je	place	nous	plaçons
tu	places	vous	placez
il	place	ils	placent
elle	place	elles	placent

Other Verbs Ending in -cer:

annoncer *to announce* **menacer** *to threaten*

avancer *to advance* **prononcer** *to pronounce*

commencer *to begin* **remplacer** *to replace*

effacer *to erase* **renoncer (à)** *to renounce*

lancer *to throw*

EXERCISE A | **Le remplaçant.** Your teacher is absent today and the students are misbehaving with the substitute teacher. Express what happens in the classroom.

1. les élèves/lancer des papiers _____

2. Carine/renoncer à faire le travail scolaire _____

3. le professeur/annoncer les devoirs _____

4. tu/menacer les autres _____

5. nous/effacer le tableau _____

6. je/avancer vers la porte _____

7. vous/prononcer mal le vocabulaire _____

8. les filles/commencer à crier _____

2. -ger Verbs

In the present tense, verbs ending in -ger insert a silent e between g and o to keep the soft g sound. Thus, the present tense form ending in -ons has a silent e inserted.

voyager *to travel*			
je	voyage	nous	voyageons
tu	voyages	vous	voyagez
il	voyage	ils	voyagent
elle	voyage	elles	voyagent

Other Verbs Ending in -*ger:*

arranger *to arrange*
bouger *to move*
changer *to change*
corriger *to correct*
déménager *to move (to another residence)*
déranger *to disturb*
diriger *to direct*
mélanger *to mix*

manger *to eat*
nager *to swim*
neiger *to snow*
obliger *to oblige, compel*
partager *to share*
plonger *to plunge, dive*
ranger *to put away; to put in order*
songer (à) *to think (of)*

EXERCISE B   **Au restaurant.** Express what each person eats for his/her main course by giving the correct form of the verb *manger.*

1. Je _____ du poisson.

2. Il _____ du rosbif.

3. Vous _____ du poulet.

4. Tu _____ du bifteck.

5. Elles _____ du canard.

6. Nous _____ de la dinde.

EXERCISE C   **L'après-midi.** Express what you and I are doing this afternoon.

EXAMPLE: corriger nos devoirs   **Nous corrigeons** nos devoirs.

1. ranger la maison   _____

2. changer les draps   _____

3. arranger les meubles   _____

4. manger des fruits   _____

5. plonger dans la piscine   _____

6. nager ensemble   _____

7. songer à nous amuser   _____

8. partager des sandwiches   _____

3.   *-yer* Verbs

In the present tense, verbs ending in *-yer* change *y* to *i* before silent *e*. (Verbs of this type are often called "shoe" verbs because the *je, tu, il, elle, ils, elles* forms, which have the same stem, have the profile of a shoe.)

nettoyer *to clean*			
je	netto*ie*	nous	nettoyons
tu	netto*ies*	vous	nettoyez
il	netto*ie*	ils	netto*ient*
elle	netto*ie*	elles	netto*ient*

Other Verbs Ending in -yer:

employer   *to use*

ennuyer   *to bore; to bother*

envoyer   *to send*

essuyer   *to wipe*

renvoyer   *to send back; to fire*

NOTE: This change of *y* to *i* is optional for verbs whose infinitive ends in *-ayer.*

essayer *to try*			
j'	essa*ie* (j'essa*ye*)	nous	essayons
tu	essa*ies* (tu essa*yes*)	vous	essayez
il	essa*ie* (il essa*ye*)	ils	essa*ient* (ils essa*yent*)
elle	essa*ie* (elle essa*ye*)	elles	essa*ient* (elles essa*yent*)

Another Verb Ending in -*ayer:*

payer   *to pay*

EXERCISE D   **En classe.** Express what each person uses in a particular class by giving the correct form of the verb *employer.*

EXAMPLE: anglais/il/stylo   Dans la classe d'anglais **il emploie** un stylo.

1. français/nous/un livre   _____

2. maths/on/une règle   _____

3. informatique/vous/un ordinateur   _____

4. dessin/tu/un crayon   _____

5. musique/elle/un piano   _____

6. biologie/ils/un microscope   _____

7. culture physique/il/un ballon   _____

8. histoire/je/une carte   _____

4. *e* + Consonant + *-er* Verbs

Verbs like *acheter* change the silent *e* to *è* in the *je, tu, il/elle, ils/elles* forms in the present tense.

acheter *to buy*			
j'	achète	nous	achetons
tu	achètes	vous	achetez
il	achète	ils	achètent
elle	achète	elles	achètent

Other *e* + Consonant + *-er* Verbs:

achever *to complete*   **lever** *to raise, to lift*
amener *to bring, to lead to*   **mener** *to lead*
élever *to bring up, to raise*   **peser** *to weigh*
emmener *to take away, to lead away*   **promener** *to walk*
enlever *to remove, to take off*   **ramener** *to bring back*
geler *to freeze*

EXERCISE E   **Les poids.**   Express how much each person weighs by giving the correct form of the verb *peser.*

EXAMPLE: Raoul/156   Raoul **pèse** cent cinquante-six livres.

1. je/120   _____
2. nous/132 _____
3. elle/97   _____
4. vous/114 _____
5. ils/145   _____
6. tu/83   _____

5. *Appeler* and *Jeter*

Two "shoe" verbs with silent *e, appeler* and *jeter,* double the consonant instead of changing *e* to *è.*

appeler *to call*			
j'	appelle	nous	appelons
tu	appelles	vous	appelez
il	appelle	ils	appellent
elle	appelle	elles	appellent

jeter *to throw*			
je	jette	nous	jettons
tu	jettes	vous	jetez
il	jette	ils	jettent
elle	jette	elles	jettent

EXERCISE F   **Les surnoms.**   Express how each person nicknames his/her child by using the correct form of the verb *appeler.*

1. J' _____ mon fils Niki.

2. Elle _____ sa fille Ronnie.

3. Nous _____ notre fils Robby.

4. Tu _____ ta fille Carie.

5. Vous _____ votre fils Arnie.

6. Ils _____ leur fille Laurie.

6.   *é* + Consonant + *-er* Verbs

Verbs with *é* in the syllable before the infinitive ending change *é* to *è* before the silent endings *-e, -es, -ent* and thus are "shoe" verbs.

célébrer *to celebrate*			
je	célèbre	nous	célébrons
tu	célèbres	vous	célébrez
il	célèbre	ils	célèbrent
elle	célèbre	elles	célèbrent

Other Verbs Ending in *é* + Consonant + *-er*

céder *to yield*   **préférer** *to prefer*

espérer *to hope*   **protéger** *to protect*

posséder *to possess, to own*   **répéter** *to repeat*

EXERCISE G   **Les desserts.**   Express the desserts each person prefers by giving the correct form of the verb *préférer.*

EXAMPLE: il/une tarte Tatin   **Il préfère** une tarte Tatin.

1. je/une glace   _____

2. vous/une crème caramel   _____

3. nous/du gâteau au chocolat _____

4. elle/une mousse au chocolat _____

5. tu/une omelette norvégienne _____

6. ils/des poires Belle Hélène _____

EXERCISE H   **Leur anniversaire.** Les Ricard are celebrating their anniversary. Complete their story by filling in the correct form of the missing verb.

amener	espérer	peser
annoncer	jeter	préférer
appeler	manger	
célébrer	payer	

Nous _____ 1. _____ une fête importante à tous nos amis. Nous _____ 2. _____ notre vingt-cinquième anniversaire de mariage. Nous _____ 3. _____ dans un bon restaurant.

Nous _____ 4. _____ tous nos amis et nous les invitons à dîner avec nous. Nous _____ 5. _____ qu'ils disent oui. Nous _____ 6. _____ nos amis au restaurant.

Nous _____ 7. _____ un coup d'oeil à la carte à l'avance parce que nous _____ 8. _____ manger le poisson. Nous ne voulons pas être déçus. Naturellement, nous _____ 9. _____ l'addition. Après cet événement, nous _____ 10. _____ tous beaucoup.

EXERCISE I   Work with a partner. Pick a holiday and discuss how you celebrate it at your home. List four things you do.

_____

_____

_____

_____

_____

EXERCISE J   **Des questions.** Answer these questions about yourself.

1. Quel genre de film préférez-vous? _____

2. Combien de CD possédez-vous? _____

3. Quand célébrez-vous votre anniversaire? _____

4. Combien pesez-vous? _____

5. Qu'est-ce que vous achetez comme cadeau à votre ami(e)? _____

6. À quelle heure commencez-vous vos devoirs généralement? _____

EXERCISE K   **Le matériel scolaire.** It's the beginning of the semester and you've gone out shopping. Write a note to your parents telling them what you are doing and what new school supplies you are buying.

_____

_____

_____

_____

_____

_____

_____

_____

_____

CHAPTER 8

Verbs Irregular in the Present Tense

The following verbs are irregular in the present tense and must be memorized.

aller	faire	pouvoir	venir
avoir	lire	prendre	voir
dire	mettre	recevoir	vouloir
écrire	ouvrir	savoir	
être	partir	sortir	

NOTE: 1. Negative, interrogative and negative interrogative constructions follow the same rules for irregular verbs as for regular ones.

Anne *n'est pas* contente.	*Anne isn't happy.*
Tu prends le bus?	*Are you taking the bus?*
*Est-ce qu'*elle vient bientôt?	*Is she coming soon?*
Dites-vous la vérité?	*Are you telling the truth?*
Tu *ne pars pas* demain?	*Aren't you leaving tomorrow?*
*Est-ce qu'*elle ne sort pas?	*Isn't she going out?*

2. Verbs that end in a vowel in the third person singular add -*t*- before the pronouns *il, elle,* or *on* to separate the vowels in the inverted interrogative construction.

Va-t-il en France?	*Is he going to France?*
A-t-elle ses papiers?	*Does she have his papers?*
Pourquoi *ouvre-t-on* la fenêtre?	*Why are they opening the window?*

1. *ALLER* To Go

je	vais	nous	allons
tu	vas	vous	allez
il/elle	va	ils/elles	vont

a. Common Expressions with *ALLER*

aller + adverb   *to feel, to be* (describing a state of health or a situation)

Comment vas-tu?	*How are you?*
Je vais très bien.	*I'm very well.*
Les affaires vont mal.	*Business is bad.*

aller à pied   *to walk, go on foot*

Nous allons à l'école à pied.	*We walk to school.*

aller à la pêche   *to go fishing*

Il va à la pêche avec son grand-père.	*He goes fishing with his grandfather.*

aller en voiture   *to go by car*
Je vais au centre commercial en voiture.   *I'm going to the mall by car.*

b. Forms of *aller* followed by an infinitive express a future action.

Il va voyager.   *He is going to travel.*

EXERCISE A   **Les voyages.**   Tell where these people are going on vacation by using the verb *aller.*

EXAMPLE: Pierre/Algérie   **Pierre *va* en Algérie.**

1. Liliane/France   _____

2. Mathieu et Yves/Belgique   _____

3. nous/Tunisie   _____

4. vous/Suisse   _____

5. je/Côte d'Ivoire   _____

6. tu/Louisiane   _____

2.   *AVOIR*   To Have

j'	ai	nous	avons
tu	as	vous	avez
il/elle	a	ils/elles	ont

a. Common Expressions with *AVOIR*

avoir...ans   *to be . . . years old*
J'ai quinze ans.   *I'm fifteen years old.*

avoir besoin de   *to need*
Il a besoin d'un stylo.   *He needs a pen.*

avoir chaud   *to be hot* (*people*).
J'ai chaud.   *I'm hot.*

avoir envie de   *to feel like; to desire, want*
Il a envie de dormir.   *He feels like sleeping*

avoir faim   *to be hungry.*
Généralement on a faim à midi.   *Generally we are hungry at noon.*

avoir froid   *to be cold* (*people*)
As-tu froid?   *Are you cold?*

avoir mal à   *to have an ache in*
J'ai mal au dos.   *I have a backache.*

avoir peur (de)   *to be afraid (of)*
As-tu peur des fantômes?   *Are you afraid of ghosts?*

avoir raison   *to be right.*
Ma mère a toujours raison.   *My mother is always right.*

avoir soif   *to be thirsty*
Quand j'ai soif je bois de l'eau.   *When I'm thirsty I drink water.*

avoir sommeil   *to be sleepy*
Le soir j'ai sommeil.   *At night I'm sleepy.*

avoir tort   *to be wrong*
Vous avez tort.   *You're wrong.*

b. Impersonal Use of *AVOIR*

il y a   *there is, there are*
y a-t-il?   *is there? are there?*
il n'y a pas   *there is not, there are not*
n'y a-t-il pas   *isn't there? aren't there?*

EXERCISE B   **Problèmes.**   Express how each person feels. Describe the problem that each person has by using *avoir* and the correct expression.

EXAMPLE: Il **a chaud.**

1. Elle _____ .   2. Nous _____ .

3. Tu _____ .   4. Vous _____ .

5. Ils _____ .   6. Je _____ .

3.   *ÊTRE* To Be

je	suis	nous	sommes
tu	es	vous	êtes
il/elle	est	ils/elles	sont

Common Expressions with *ÊTRE*

être à *to belong to*

Ce livre est à moi.   *This book belongs to me. (This book is mine.)*

être en train de *to be in the process of*

Je suis en train de lire.   *I'm reading.*

EXERCISE C   **Les contraires.**   The information you've been given is wrong. Give the
correct form of the verb *être* and an antonym for each word.

EXAMPLE: il/faible.   Il n'est pas faible. Au contraire, il est **fort.**

1. je/grand   _____

2. nous/pauvres _____

3. elle/laide   _____

4. tu/paresseux _____

5. vous/égoïste _____

6. ils/heureux _____

4.   *FAIRE*   To Make, To Do

je	fais	nous	faisons
tu	fais	vous	faites
il/elle	fait	ils/elles	font

Common Expressions with *FAIRE*

faire attention (à)   *to pay attention (to)*
Il *fait* attention au prof.   *He pays attention to the teacher.*

faire des courses   *to go shopping*
Maman *fait* des courses chaque jour.   *Mom goes shopping every day.*

faire une promenade   *to go for a walk*
Ils *font* une promenade.   *They are going for a walk.*

faire un voyage (en avion, en voiture)   *to take a trip (by plane, by car)*
La famille Dupont *fait* un voyage   *The Dupont family is taking*
  en avion.   *a plane trip.*

FAIRE + weather expressions

Quel temps fait-il?	*What's the weather?*
Il fait beau.	*It's nice weather.*
Il fait mauvais.	*It's bad weather.*
Il fait froid.	*It's cold.*
Il fait chaud.	*It's warm, hot.*
Il fait frais.	*It's cool.*
Il fait du vent.	*It's windy.*
Il fait du soleil.	*It's sunny.*

FAIRE + sports
Nous faisons du tennis.   *We play tennis.*

EXERCISE D   **Les sports.**   Tell what sport each person is playing.

1. J'achète des joggers. Je _____ .

2. Nous achetons une bicyclette. Nous _____ .

3. Elles achètent des clubs de golf. Elles _____ .

4. Vous achetez une raquette et des balles. Vous _____ .

5. Il achète un gant et une batte. Il _____ .

6. Tu achètes des bâtons et des skis. Tu _____ .

5.   *METTRE*   To Put (On)

je	mets	nous	mettons
tu	mets	vous	mettez
il/elle	met	ils/elles	mettent

Other verbs conjugated like *METTRE:*

permettre *to allow*   **remettre** *to put back; to deliver*

EXERCISE E   **Les vêtements.**   Write what each person puts on for the weather conditions they encounter. Use the verb *mettre.*

1. Quand il fait froid nous _____ .

2. Quand il fait frais il _____ .

3. Quand il fait du vent je _____ .

4. Quand il fait du soleil tu _____ .

5. Quand il neige elles _____ .

6. Quand il pleut vous _____ .

6.   *OUVRIR*   To Open

j'	ouvre	nous	ouvrons
tu	ouvres	vous	ouvrez
il/elle	ouvre	ils/elles	ouvrent

Other verbs conjugated like *OUVRIR:*

couvrir *to cover*   **découvrir** *to discover*

EXERCISE F   **Le courrier.**   Express what each person opens. Use the verb *ouvrir.*

1. nous/le paquet   _____

2. ils/la boîte   _____

3. elle/le télégramme   _____

4. vous/la lettre   _____

5. je/l'aérogramme   _____

6. tu/l'enveloppe   _____

7.   *PRENDRE*   To Take

je	prends	nous	prenons
tu	prends	vous	prenez
il/elle	prend	ils/elles	prennent

Other verbs conjugated like *PRENDRE:*

apprendre *to learn*   **comprendre** *to understand*

EXERCISE G   **Les langues étrangères.**   Express which language each person understands. Use the verb *comprendre* and the appropriate noun from the list below.

l'allemand	l'espagnol	l'italien
le chinois	le français	le russe

1. Mario est de Rome. Il _____ .

2. Je suis de Hong Kong. Je _____ .

3. Olga et Galina sont de Moscou. Elles _____ .

4. Nous sommes de Berlin. Nous _____ .

5. Vous êtes de Nice. Vous _____ .

6. Tu es de Madrid. Tu _____ .

8.   *RECEVOIR*   To Receive

je	reçois	nous	recevons
tu	reçois	vous	recevez
il/elle	reçoit	ils/elles	reçoivent

EXERCISE H   **Les cadeaux.**   Indicate what each person receives as a gift by giving the correct form of the verb *recevoir.*

EXAMPLE: Jean **reçoit** des CD.

des fleurs	des bijoux
une carte	des vêtements
une boîte de chocolats	des CD
de l'argent	

1. Paul et Robert _____

2. je _____

3. Marie _____

4. tu _____

5. vous _____

6. nous _____

9.   *SAVOIR*   To Know (How)

je	sais	nous	savons
tu	sais	vous	savez
il/elle	sait	ils/elles	savent

EXERCISE I   **Une nouvelle.**   A new girl just arrived in your class. Use the verb *savoir* to tell what the different people know about her.

EXAMPLE: François / son nom de famille   François **sait** son nom de famille.

1. tu / ses coordonnées _____

2. nous/son prénom _____

3. ils/sa nationalité _____

4. elle/son âge _____

5. je/son adresse _____

6. vous/sa date de naissance _____

10.   *VENIR*   To Come

je	viens	nous	venons
tu	viens	vous	venez
il/elle	vient	ils/elles	viennent

Other verbs conjugated like *VENIR:*

devenir *to become*   **revenir** *to come back*

EXERCISE J   **Les métiers.**   Tell what the people become after finishing school. Use the verb *devenir* and the list below to complete the sentence. Make any necessary agreement for a feminine or plural subject.

EXAMPLE: Il aime combattre le feu.   **Il devient pompier.**

artiste	chef	garçon
boucher	coiffeur	programmeur

1. J'aime dessiner et faire de la peinture. Je _____ .

2. Nous aimons couper et coiffer les cheveux. Nous _____ .

3. Elle aime travailler avec l'ordinateur. Elle _____ .

4. Vous aimez cuisiner. Vous _____ .

5. Tu aimes servir les repas. Tu _____ .

6. Ils aiment vendre la viande. Ils _____ .

11.   *VOIR*   To See

je	vois	nous	voyons
tu	vois	vous	voyez
il/elle	voit	ils/elles	voient

EXERCISE K   **Au zoo.**   Express what each person sees at the zoo.

EXAMPLE: Il **voit des gorilles.**

éléphants	tigres	lions
girafes	zèbres	rhinocéros

1. nous _____

2. tu _____

3. ils _____

4. vous _____

5. elle _____

6. je _____

12.   *POUVOIR*   To Be Able To, Can / *VOULOIR*   To Want

je	peux	nous	pouvons
tu	peux	vous	pouvez
il/elle	peut	ils/elles	peuvent

je	veux	nous	voulons
tu	veux	vous	voulez
il/elle	veut	ils/elles	veulent

EXERCISE L   **Objets perdus.**   Write what each person wants to do but can't because he/she can't find something. Use the verbs *vouloir* and *pouvoir*.

EXAMPLE: il/faire ses devoirs/son livre

Il **veut** faire ses devoirs mais il ne **peut** pas trouver son livre.

1. je/lire/mes lunettes   _____

2. nous/écouter de la musique/trouver nos CD   _____

3. elle/conduire/trouver les clefs de la voiture   _____

4. tu/payer l'addition au restaurant/ton argent   _____

5. vous/téléphoner à un ami/votre cellulaire   _____

6. ils/faire du golf/leurs clubs   _____

13.   *PARTIR* To Leave, Go Away / *SORTIR* To Go Out

je	pars	nous	partons
tu	pars	vous	partez
il/elle	part	ils/elles	partent

je	sors	nous	sortons
tu	sors	vous	sortez
il/elle	sort	ils/elles	sortent

EXERCISE M   **On sort.**   Tell at what time each person is leaving and with whom they are going out.   Use the verbs *partir* and *sortir*.

EXAMPLE: il/10/Renée

Il **part** à dix heures et il **sort** avec Renée.

1. vous/11:30/Christophe   _____

2. tu/1:45/Danielle   _____

3. ils/3:10/Lucien   _____

4. je/4:55/Patrick   _____

5. elle/5:35/Raymond   _____

6. nous/6:20/Gisèle   _____

14.   *DIRE* To Say / *ÉCRIRE* To Write / *LIRE* To Read

je	dis	nous	disons
tu	dis	vous	dites
il/elle	dit	ils/elles	disent

j'	écris	nous	écrivons
tu	écris	vous	écrivez
il/elle	écrit	ils/elles	écrivent

je	lis	nous	lisons
tu	lis	vous	lisez
il/elle	lit	ils/elles	lisent

EXERCISE N | **Lettres d'amour.** Express what each person writes in his/her love letter. Use the verb *écrire.*

EXAMPLE: il   **Il écrit,** "Tu es si jolie."

Je t'aime.   Je pense toujours à toi.
Tu es formidable.   Je rêve de toi.
Je suis fou (folle) de toi.   Tu es le garçon (la fille) de mes rêves.

1. ils   _____

2. nous   _____

3. vous   _____

4. je   _____

5. elle   _____

6. tu   _____

EXERCISE O | **Une journée malheureuse.** Hervé has to go somewhere today. Complete his story with the appropriate form of the verbs indicated.

J' _____ un rendez-vous cet après-midi et je ne _____ pas du tout
          1. (avoir)   2. (être)

content. Je _____ qu'il faut être heureux quand on _____ . Quand
              3. (savoir)   4. (sortir)

même, je ne _____ pas sortir mais je ne _____ pas rester à la maison.
             5. (vouloir)   6. (pouvoir)

Il _____ froid dehors et je _____ mon manteau d'hiver. À contrecoeur,
   7. (faire)   8. (mettre)

je _____ de ma maison à midi. Je _____ le métro, qui
   9. (partir)   10. (prendre)

_____ drôlement vite. J'arrive devant un grand bâtiment et j' _____ la
 11. (aller)   12. (ouvrir)

porte. Je _____ le bureau où on m'attend. J'entre et j' _____ mon nom
           13. (voir)   14. (écrire)

sur une longue liste. Je _____ mon livre et je _____ . Une demi-heure
                          15. (sortir)   16. (lire)

passe et je ne _____ plus me concentrer sur mon livre. Tout d'un coup une femme
               17. (pouvoir)

_____ et elle _____ , "Hervé Brun, entrez s'il vous plaît." En ce mo-
 18. (venir)   19. (dire)

ment-là, j' _____ très peur. _____ -vous pourquoi? C'est aujourd'hui
            20. (avoir)   21. (savoir)

que j' _____ mon examen annuel chez mon dentiste.
        22. (avoir)

| EXERCISE P | **Les accomplissements.** Work with a partner. Discuss and then list four things you know how to do. |

_____

_____

_____

_____

_____

_____

_____

| EXERCISE Q | **Une journée libre.** Write a composition about what you do on a day off from school. Mention activities that you want to do as well as those you are in the habit of doing. |

_____

_____

_____

_____

_____

_____

_____

CHAPTER 9

Imperative

The imperative is a verb form used to give commands or suggestions.

1. Imperative of Regular Verbs

a. Most forms of the imperative are the same as the corresponding forms of the present tense, except for the omission of the subject pronouns *tu*, *vous*, and *nous*.

FAMILIAR		FORMAL/PLURAL		FIRST PERSON PLURAL	
Étudie!	*Study!*	**Étudiez!**	*Study!*	**Étudions!**	*Let's study!*
Choisis!	*Choose!*	**Choisissez!**	*Choose!*	**Choisissons!**	*Let's choose!*
Attends!	*Wait!*	**Attendez!**	*Wait!*	**Attendons!**	*Let's wait!*

> **NOTE:** The familiar imperative of *-er* verbs drops the final *-s* of the present tense forms.
>
> **Tu parles français.** *You speak French.*
> **Parle français!** *Speak French!*

b. In the negative imperative, *ne* and the negative word surround the verb.

*N'*oublie **pas** la date! *Don't forget the date!*
Ne mangez **rien!** *Don't eat anything!*
Ne marchons **plus!** *Let's not walk any more!*

2. Imperative of Irregular Verbs

The imperative of irregular verbs generally follows the same pattern as regular verbs.

aller *to go*	**va, allez, allons**
faire *to do*	**fais, faites, faisons**
venir *to come*	**viens, venez, venons**

> **NOTE:** 1. Verbs conjugated like *-er* verbs in the present tense and the verb *aller* drop the final *-s* in the familiar command form.
>
> **Ouvre la lettre!** *Open the letter!*
> **Va au magasin!** *Go to the store!*
>
> 2. The verbs *avoir, être,* and *savoir* have irregular forms in the imperative.
>
> **avoir** *to have* **aie, ayez, ayons**
> **être** *to be* **sois, soyez, soyons**
> **savoir** *to know* **sache, sachez, sachons**

EXERCISE A   **Une salade française.**   Tell a friend how to prepare a *salade Niçoise.*

EXAMPLE: aller au marché   **Va au marché.**

1. choisir des tomates, des pommes de terre et des haricots verts frais

   _____

2. laver les légumes

   _____

3. couper les tomates

   _____

4. faire cuire les haricots verts et les pommes de terre

   _____

5. mettre les légumes dans un saladier

   _____

6. ajouter du thon

   _____

7. couvrir la salade de vinaigrette

   _____

8. manger la salade

   _____

EXERCISE B   **Un boulot.**   Your friend is looking for a job and you want to give some good advice about how to act at an interview. What do you say?

EXAMPLE: (perdre) **Ne perds pas** patience.

1. (être)   _____ timide.
2. (mâcher)   _____ de chewing gum.
3. (parlez)   _____ trop.
4. (mettre)   _____ de vieux vêtements.
5. (arriver)   _____ en retard.
6. (avoir)   _____ peur.

EXERCISE C   **Un régime.**   Your friends are all on a diet. What advice do you give them?

EXAMPLE: limiter la consommation de calories   **Limitez** la consommation de calories.

1. rester actifs   _____
2. manger beaucoup de salade   _____

3. prendre des vitamines _____

4. oublier les desserts _____

5. faire de l'exercice aérobic _____

6. marcher beaucoup. _____

EXERCISE D | **Un dîner spécial.** Special guests are being entertained for dinner this evening at home. The children want to know what is expected of them. Express the warnings given to the children.

EXAMPLE: On mange vite? **Ne mangez pas** vite!

1. On joue dans le salon? _____

2. On écoute la musique avant le dîner? _____

3. On descend avant l'heure du dîner? _____

4. On allume la télé pendant le dîner? _____

5. On fait beaucoup de bruit? _____

6. On interrompt la conversation des adultes? _____

EXERCISE E | **La retraite.** Your teacher is retiring. Express the suggestions made by your classmates to honor your teacher.

EXAMPLE: apporter des cartes **Apportons** des cartes.

1. acheter un cadeau _____

2. dire,"au revoir" _____

3. faire une fête en classe _____

4. écrire des lettres de gratitude _____

5. préparer un gâteau _____

6. inviter sa famille _____

EXERCISE F | **Épargnons de l'argent!** M. Robert and his wife are saving to buy a new house. Express their suggestion for saving money.

EXAMPLE: dépenser trop **Ne dépensons pas** trop.

1. aller au cinéma trop souvent _____

2. acheter beaucoup de choses inutiles _____

3. dîner au restaurant tout le temps _____

4. voyager à l'étranger   _____

5. sortir souvent   _____

6. utiliser notre carte de crédit _____

EXERCISE G   **La mousse au chocolat.**   Read this recipe for a delicious dessert. Then answer the following questions.

> ### Les ingrédients
>
> 8 oz. de chocolat demi-sucré   2 œufs séparés
> 1 oz. de chocolat non-sucré   2 tasses de crème
> 2 grandes cuillerées de beurre   2 grandes cuillerées de café noir
>
> La recette
> Faites fondre le chocolat demi-sucré, le chocolat non-sucré et le beurre à feu doux. Remuez. Enlevez le chocolat du feu. Laissez refroidir le chocolat. Ajoutez le café et les jaunes d'œufs. Battez les blanc d'œufs en neige ferme. Fouettez la crème. Incorporez les blancs d'œufs au chocolat. Puis incorporez la crème fouettée. Mettez la mousse dans des bols individuels et laissez-la refroidir pendant quatre heures. Servez avec de la crème fouettée.

1. What are the ingredients of this recipe?

2. What do you do to the chocolate?

3. Which ingredient is mixed with the chocolate first?

4. What do you have to do with the chocolate mixture before adding the coffee and egg yolks?

5. What do you do to the egg whites?

6. What do you do to the cream?

7. What gets added to the chocolate after the coffee and the egg yolks?

8. Where do you put the mousse to make individual portions?

9. How long does the mousse have to cool?

10. What do you serve with the mousse?

EXERCISE H   Work with a partner.   Take turns giving each other commands that can be done in class and then carry them out.

_____

_____

_____

_____

_____

| EXERCISE I | **Les conseils.** Your friend is having trouble passing math and needs some advice. Write a note giving your suggestions for doing well in the class.

_____

_____

_____

_____

_____

CHAPTER 10
Articles and Nouns

1. Forms of the Definite Article

a. In English, the definite article is always "the". In French, the definite article has four forms: *le, la, l', les*.

	MASCULINE	FEMININE
SINGULAR	*le* livre *l'*ami	*la* règle *l'*amie
PLURAL	*les* livres *les* amis	*les* règles *les* amies

> **NOTE:** 1. The form *l'* is used before a singular noun of either gender beginning with a vowel or silent *h*.
>
> 2. In French, the article is expressed before each noun, even though it may be omitted in English.
>
> **les** hommes et **les** femmes   (*the*) *men and women*

b. The prepositions *à* and *de* contract with *le* and *les* becoming *au* and *aux*, *du* and *des* respectively.

à + *le* garçon = *au* garçon	*to the boy*
à + *les* femmes = *aux* femmes	*to the women*
de + *le* garçon = *du* garçon	*of the boy*
de + *les* femmes = *des* femmes	*of the women*

> **NOTE:** There is no contraction with *la* or *l'*.

c. The definite article is used when one wants to indicate a specific being or thing (*le bureau*), as in English (the office). It is also used in the following constructions where English does not use the article.

(1) With nouns used in a general or abstract sense.

J'aime *la pâtisserie.*   *I like pastry.*

(2) With names of languages and school subjects, except directly after *parler*, after *en*, and in an adjective phrase with *de*.

J'étudie *le français.*	*I study French.*
Le français **est facile.**	*French is easy.*
Je parle bien *le français.*	*I speak French well.*
But:	
Je *parle français.*	*I speak French.*

Ce film est *en français*.   *This film is in French.*
C'est mon prof *de français*.   *It's my French teacher.*

(3) In place of the possessive adjective, with parts of the body when the possessor is clear.

Il lève *la main*.   *He raises his hand.*

(4) With days of the week in a plural sense.

Le samedi je range ma chambre.   *On Saturday(s) I straighten my room.*

(5) With names of seasons except after the preposition *en*.

Il fait frais en automne et au printemps.   *It's cool in the fall and in winter.*

(6) With dates.

C'est mardi, *le seize juillet*.   *It's Tuesday, July 16th.*

(7) With names of most countries except after the preposition *en*.

La France est *en Europe*.   *France is in Europe.*

(8) In certain common expressions:

à l'école	*to (in) school*
à la maison	*at home, home*
le matin	*in the morning*
l'après-midi	*in the afternoon*
le soir	*in the evening*
le week-end	*on the weekend*
le mois prochain	*next month*
la semaine dernière	*last week*
l'année passée	*last year*
l'été prochain	*next summer*

EXERCISE A   **Une école spécialisée.** Mme Druard is taking special courses. Read her story and fill in the appropriate definite article where it is necessary. If it is not necessary, leave a blank.

———— cuisine est ma pièce favorite à ———— maison. Pourquoi? Parce que j'adore faire
  1.   2.

———— pâtisseries. Je vais à ———— école de cuisine, Grands Chefs du Monde, où j'apprends
  3.   4.

beaucoup. Nous avons classe ———— lundi après-midi. ———— professeurs sont vraiment
                              5.   6.

formidables. ———— recettes, en général, sont en ———— anglais, mais quelquefois, elles sont
              7.   8.

en ———— français. Mon professeur préféré, M. Lelong, parle très bien ———— français et
    9.   10.

alors, il traduit ——— recettes pour ——— membres du groupe. À ——— maison, ma
                   11.   12.   13.

famille est toujours très contente. Tout ——— monde adore ——— chocolat et ma spécialité
                                        14.   15.

est ——— gâteau au chocolat.
     16.

2.   Forms of the Indefinite Article

a. The indefinite singular article in French has two forms, *un* and *une,* corresponding
to the English *a (an).* It refers to beings and things not specifically identified (a friend,
any friend, not the friend you go to school with). The plural form is *des* (some, any).

ARTICLE	USED BEFORE	EXAMPLE	MEANING
un	masculine singular nouns	un sac à dos	a backpack
une	feminine singular nouns	une trousse	a pencil case
des	all plural nouns	des crayons	some pencils

b. The indefinite article is omitted in the following cases.

(1) After *être* and *devenir* with unmodified names of nationalities, occupations, or
professions.

Elle est italienne.   *She is an Italian.*
Il devient docteur.   *He is becoming a doctor.*

NOTE: The article is used if the noun is modified or when *c'est* is used.

Il est un bon professeur.   *He's a good teacher.*
C'est un professeur.   *He's a teacher.*

(2) After exclamatory adjectives *quel, quels, quelle, quelles.*

Quelle belle voiture!   *What a beautiful car!*

(3) Before the numbers *cent* and *mille.*

cent euros   *one hundred euros*
mille personnes   *one thousand people*

EXERCISE B   **Une famille.**   Read the story of Mme Chénier. Fill in the indefinite article
where it is necessary. If it is not necessary, leave a blank.

Mme Chénier est ——— française. Elle a ——— mari. Il est ——— programmeur. Il est ——— si
                 1.   2.   3.   4.

bon programmeur qu'il reçoit ——— mille dollars par semaine. Mme Chénier travaille aussi.
                             5.

Elle est ——— professeur extraordinaire. Mais aussi, elle est ——— auteur de livres scolaires.
         6.   7.

Les Chénier ont ——— fille et ——— fils. Ils habitent ——— jolie maison en ville.
                8.   9.   10.

3.   Forms of the Partitive Article

The partitive article expresses an indefinite quantity or part of a whole (some, any). It is expressed in French by *de* + the definite article.

ARTICLE	USED BEFORE	EXAMPLE	MEANING
du	masculine singular nouns beginning with a consonant	**du gâteau**	*some cake*
de la	feminine singular nouns beginning with a consonant	**de la glace**	*some ice cream*
de l'	singular nouns beginning with a vowel	**de l'eau**	*some (any) water*
des	all plural nouns	**des tartes**	*some tarts*

a. Unlike English, where *some* may be omitted, the partitive article may not be omitted in French and is repeated before each noun.

Je prends *du* pain et *du* beurre.   *I'll take some bread and butter.*

b. When an adjective precedes a plural noun, *des* is usually replaced by *de* (*d'* before a vowel or silent *h*).

Elle cuisine *de* bons repas.   *She cooks good meals.*

c. When a plural adjective is part of a noun compound, the form *des* is used.

***des* grands-parents**   *grandparents*

d. In a negative sentence partitive articles become *de* before a direct object:

Il ne mange pas de viande.   *He doesn't eat meat.*

EXERCISE C   **Qu'est-ce qu'il y a dans le frigo?**   Look at the refrigerator at the Dupont home. Indicate what is in the fridge and what is not.

fruits
crème
pain
œufs
beurre
glace
eau minérale
tomates
orangeade
poisson
céréales
chocolat
lait
fromage

EXAMPLE: **Il y a du lait.**   **Il n'y a pas de chocolat.**

1. Il y a _____ .
2. Il y a _____ .
3. Il y a _____ .
4. Il y a _____ .
5. Il y a _____ .
6. Il y a _____ .
7. Il y a _____ .

8. Il n'y a pas _____ .
9. Il n'y a pas _____ .
10. Il n'y a pas _____ .
11. Il n'y a pas _____ .
12. Il n'y a pas _____ .
13. Il n'y a pas _____ .
14. Il n'y a pas _____ .

4.   Demonstrative Adjectives

Demonstrative adjectives point out the object or person referred to (this, that, these, those). They precede and agree with the nouns they modify.

ARTICLE	USED BEFORE	EXAMPLE	MEANING
ce	a masculine singular noun beginning with a consonant	**ce garçon**	*this (that) boy*
cet	a masculine singular noun beginning with a vowel	**cet homme**	*this (that) man*
cette	a feminine singular noun	**cette femme**	*this (that) woman*
ces	all plural nouns	**ces gens**	*these (those) people*

NOTE: 1.   The demonstrative adjective is repeated before each noun.

ces **robes et** *cette* **jupe**   *these (those) dresses and this (that) skirt*

2.   To distinguish between this and that or between these and those, *-ci* and *-là* are placed, with hyphens, after the nouns being contrasted. For this or these, *-ci* is added; for that or those, *-là* is added.

cette fille-*ci* **ou cette fille-***là*   *this girl or that girl*
ces livres-*ci* **ou ces livres-***là*   *these books or those books*

EXERCISE D   **Les prix.**   Ask the cost of each item you will need to redecorate your bedroom.

EXAMPLE: C'est combien **cette télévision?**

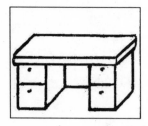

1. _____

2. _____

3. _____

4. _____

5. _____

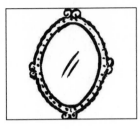

6. _____

| EXERCISE E | **De nouveaux vêtements.**   You are shopping with a friend. Ask which item he/she prefers. |

EXAMPLE: (robe)   Tu préfères **cette robe-ci ou cette robe-là?**

1. (imperméable)   _____

2. (pantalon)   _____

3. (bottes)   _____

4. (chemise)   _____

5.   Gender of Nouns

French nouns are either masculine or feminine. There are no general rules to determine the gender of all nouns, but the gender of many nouns can be determined by their meaning or their ending. The gender of other nouns must be learned individually.

a. Nouns that refer to males are masculine. Nouns that refer to females are feminine.

MASCULINE		FEMININE	
le garçon	_the boy_	**la fille**	_the girl_

b. The gender of some nouns may be determined by their ending.

MASCULINE		FEMININE	
-acle	spect*acle*	-ade	citronn*ade*
-age*	vill*age*	-ale	capit*ale*
-al	journ*al*	-ance	ch*ance*
-eau*	bur*eau*	-ence	ag*ence*
-et	cabin*et*	-ette	raqu*ette*
-ier	pap*ier*	-ie	mag*ie*
-isme	cycl*isme*	-ique	informat*ique*
-ment	change*ment*	-oire	gl*oire*
		-sion	ver*sion*
		-tion	na*tion*
		-ure	coiff*ure*

*Note these exceptions, which are all feminine: _la page, la plage; l'eau, la peau_

c. Some feminine nouns are formed by adding *e* to the masculine.

MASCULINE	FEMININE	MEANING
l'ami	l'amie	*friend*
l'étudiant	l'étudiante	*student*
le voisin	la voisine	*neighbor*

d. Some feminine nouns are formed by changing the masculine ending to a feminine ending.

	MASCULINE		FEMININE	MEANING
-an	pays*an*	-anne	pays*anne*	*peasant*
-el	contractu*el*	-elle	contractu*elle*	*meter reader*
-er	bouch*er*	-ère	bouch*ère*	*butcher*
-eur	vend*eur*	-euse	vend*euse*	*sales person*
-ien	music*ien*	-ienne	music*ienne*	*musician*
-ier	pâtiss*ier*	-ière	pâtiss*ière*	*pastry chef*
-on	patr*on*	-onne	patr*onne*	*boss*
-teur	specta*teur*	-trice	specta*trice*	*spectator*

e. Some nouns have the same form in the masculine and the feminine.

l'artiste	*artist*	l'enfant	*child*
le (la) camarade	*friend*	le (la) secrétaire	*secretary*
l'élève	*student*	le (la) touriste	*tourist*

f. Some nouns are always masculine or feminine regardless of the gender of the person referred to.

ALWAYS MASCULINE		ALWAYS FEMININE	
l'agent de police	*police officer*	la personne	*person*
le bébé	*baby*	la victime	*victime*
le chef	*chef, cook, chief, head*		
le médecin	*doctor*		
le professeur	*teacher, professor*		

EXERCISE F   **Masculin ou féminin.** You are having a vocabulary quiz in your French class. Put *un* or *une* in front of each word to indicate that you know the gender of the word.

1. _____ trompette

2. _____ présence

3. _____ changement

4. _____ débacle

5. _____ bougie

6. _____ livret

7. _____ animal

8. _____ chance

9. _____ cathédrale

10. _____ boutique

11. _____ gâteau

12. _____ garage

13. _____ limonade

14. _____ histoire

EXERCISE G   **Le travail.** Both parents in the family have the same job. Express the job of the other parent.

1. M. Cousteau est programmeur et Mme Cousteau est _____ .

2. Mme Étienne est pâtissière et M. Étienne est _____ .

3. M. Marché est professeur et Mme Marché est _____ .

4. Mme Lavigne est opticienne et M. Lavigne est _____ .

5. M. Duchamp est acteur et Mme Duchamp est _____ .

6. Mme Manet est boulangère et M. Manet est _____ .

7. M. Daudet est agent de police et Mme Daudet est _____ .

8. Mme Aimé est patronne et M. Aimé est _____ .

6.   Plural of Nouns

a. The plural of most French nouns is formed by adding _s_ to the singular.

SINGULAR		PLURAL	
le livre	_the book_	**les livres**	_the books_
un stylo	_a pen_	**des stylos**	_some pens_
cette gomme	_this eraser_	**ces gommes**	_these erasers_

b. Nouns ending is -s, -x, or -z remain unchanged in the plural.

SINGULAR		PLURAL	
un autobus	_a bus_	**des autobus**	_some buses_
cette voix	_this voice_	**ces voix**	_these voices_
le nez	_the nose_	**les nez**	_the noses_

c. Nouns ending in *–eau* and *–eu* add *x* in the plural.

SINGULAR		PLURAL	
un gâteau	*a cake*	**des gâteaux**	*some cakes*
le feu	*the fire*	**les feux**	*the fires*

d. Nouns ending in *–al* change *–al* to *–aux* in the plural.

l'animal (*m.*)	*the animal*	**les animaux**	*the animals*

e. Some nouns have irregular plurals.

SINGULAR		PLURAL	
l'œil (*m.*)	*eye*	**les yeux**	*eyes*
madame	*Madam, Mrs.*	**mesdames**	*ladies*
mademoiselle	*Miss*	**mesdemoiselles**	*Misses*
monsieur	*gentleman, Mr.*	**messieurs**	*gentlemen*

f. A few names are used mainly in the plural.

les gens (*m.* or *f.*)	*people*	**les mathématiques** (*f.*)	*mathematics*
les lunettes (*f.*)	*eyeglasses*	**les vacances** (*f.*)	*vacation*

g. Family names do not add *s* in the plural.

les Leclerc

EXERCISE H **Le déménagement.** The Souper family is moving. Express what they find in the attic.

EXAMPLE: Un couteau? (2)   Mais non, **deux couteaux.**

1. Un jeu? (11) _____

2. Un tapis? (3) _____

3. Un chapeau? (5) _____

4. Un journal? (15) _____

5. Une croix? (4) _____

6. Un bijou? (12) _____

7. Nouns of Quantity

Nouns that express quantity or measure are followed by *de* alone before another noun. Some common nouns of quantity are:

une boîte	*a box*	**un paquet**	*a package*
une bouteille	*a bottle*	**un sac**	*a bag*
une douzaine	*a dozen*	**une tasse**	*a cup*

une paire	*a pair*	**un verre**	*a glass*

Une boîte *de* chocolats est un bon cadeau.   *A box of chocolate is a nice gift.*

EXERCISE I   **Chez l'épicier.** Express what items are on Chantal's shopping list.

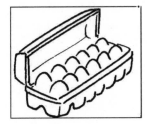

1. _____

2. _____

3. _____

4. _____

5. _____

EXERCISE J | **Une annonce.** Read the ad and then write a list of what you would expect to be able to buy in this store.

> *Paris Souvenir*
> *Fabrication et vente de souvenirs*
> *Spécialiste en articles de Paris*
> *6 rue Corot 16ᵉ*

1. _____
2. _____
3. _____
4. _____
5. _____
6. _____

EXERCISE K | **Les professions.** Work with a partner and talk about the professions of people you know.

_____
_____
_____
_____
_____

EXERCISE L | **Une fête.** You are planning a party. Write a note to your parents telling them what you need for it.

_____
_____
_____
_____
_____

CHAPTER 11
Object, Relative, and Stress Pronouns

1. Direct Object Pronouns

a. Forms

SINGULAR		PLURAL	
me (m')	*me*	**nous**	*we*
te (t')	*you (familiar)*	**vous**	*you (also formal singular)*
le (l')	*him, it (masculine)*	**les**	*them*
la (l')	*her, it (feminine)*	**les**	*them*

b. Uses

A direct object pronoun replaces a direct object noun and answers the question *whom?* or *what?*

J'aime Raymond.	*I like Raymond.*
Je *l'*aime.	*I like him*
Nous préparons cette recette.	*We prepare that recipe.*
Nous *la* préparons.	*We prepare it.*
Elle trouve ses clefs.	*She finds her keys.*
Elle *les* trouve.	*She finds them.*

> NOTE: Verbs like *attendre* (to wait for), *écouter* (to listen to), *chercher* (to look for), *demander* (to ask for), *payer* (to pay for), and *regarder* (to look at) take a direct object in French.
>
> | **J'attends mes amis.** | *I wait for my friends.* |
> |---|---|
> | **Je *les* attends.** | *I wait for them.* |

c. Position

1. The direct object pronoun precedes the words *voici* (here is, here are) and *voilà* (there is, there are).

***La* voilà.**	*There she (it) is.*

2. The direct object pronoun normally precedes the verb of which it is the object.

Je *le* prends.	*I'll take it.*
Il ne *les* attend pas.	*He isn't waiting for them.*
***La* cherches-tu?**	*Are you looking for it?*

| EXERCISE A | **Les travaux domestiques.** You and a friend are discussing how you help around the house. Write your conversation. |

EXAMPLE: débarasser la table

VOTRE AMI: **La** débarrasses-tu?

VOUS: Je **la** débarrasse.

VOTRE AMI: Moi, je ne **la** débarrasse pas.

1. nettoyer la maison

    VOTRE AMI: _____

    VOUS: _____

    VOTRE AMI: _____

2. faire les courses

    VOTRE AMI: _____

    VOUS: _____

    VOTRE AMI: _____

3. passer l'aspirateur

    VOTRE AMI: _____

    VOUS: _____

    VOTRE AMI: _____

4. garder les enfants

    VOTRE AMI: _____

    VOUS: _____

    VOTRE AMI: _____

5. laver la vaisselle

    VOTRE AMI: _____

    VOUS: _____

    VOTRE AMI: _____

6. mettre le couvert

    VOTRE AMI: _____

    VOUS: _____

    VOTRE AMI: _____

3. When a pronoun is the direct object of an infinitive, the pronoun precedes the infinitive.

Il veut *me* **voir.**	*He wants to see me.*
Je ne veux pas *le* **voir.**	*I don't want to see him.*
Veux-tu *me* **voir?**	*Do you want to see me?*

EXERCISE B   **Les promesses.**   You promise your parents that your grades will improve. For each of the following, write your parents' questions and your affirmative or negative answer.

EXAMPLE: écouter le prof (oui)   déranger les autres (non)
   Vas-tu l'écouter?   **Vas-tu les déranger?**
   Oui, je vais l'écouter.   **Non, je ne vais pas les déranger.**

1. copier les notes (oui)

   _____

   _____

2. perdre ton manuel scolaire (non)

   _____

   _____

3. rater les examens (non)

   _____

   _____

4. apporter les livres nécessaires en classe (oui)

   _____

   _____

5. étudier la grammaire (oui)

   _____

   _____

6. oublier les devoirs à la maison (non)

   _____

   _____

EXERCISE C   **Les copains.**   Express what these friends do to help each other at school by putting the pronoun in its proper place.

EXAMPLE: (nous) il appelle tout le temps
   Il **nous** appelle tout le temps.

1. (le) voilà en train d'expliquer le vocabulaire à Charles

   _____

2. (me) Christophe aide

   _____

3. (la) nous aimons bien parce qu'elle pose de bonnes questions

   _____

4. (nous) il va inviter à étudier chez lui

   _____

5. (les) Paul écoute toujours

   _____

6. (te) dérange-t-il quand il est impatient

   _____

7. (la) allez-vous protéger quand elle fait des erreurs

   _____

8. (vous) Renée ne veut pas corriger souvent

   _____

4. In an affirmative command, the direct object pronoun follows the verb and is attached to it by a hyphen. The pronouns _me_ and _te_ change to _moi_ and _toi_ after the verb. In a negative command, the object pronoun retains its usual position before the verb.

AFFIRMATIVE COMMAND		NEGATIVE COMMAND	
Cherche-le.	_Look for it._	**Ne le cherche pas.**	_Don't look for it._
Écoutez-moi.	_Listen to me._	**Ne m'écoutez pas.**	_Don't listen to me._

EXERCISE D | **Le départ.** The Hyppolites are going on vacation. Mme Hyppolite is very nervous. Write what she says to her husband about things she's misplaced.

EXAMPLE: les clefs

Cherche-les.

Les voilà.

Ne les cherche pas.

1. l'itinéraire

   _____

   _____

   _____

2. les chèques de voyage

_____

_____

_____

3. la valise bleue

_____

_____

_____

4. les passeports

_____

_____

_____

EXERCISE E   **L'indécision.**   Alberte is thinking about going out. At first she doesn't want to be bothered by anyone but then she changes her mind. Express what she tells her friends.

EXAMPLE: inviter   **Ne m' invitez pas.**
                              Oh, invitez-moi.

1. accompagner

_____

_____

2. écouter

_____

_____

3. appeler

_____

_____

4. chercher

_____

_____

2.   Indirect Object Pronouns

a. The forms of indirect object pronouns are the same as those of direct object pronouns, except for the third person singular (*lui*) and the third person plural (*leur*).

SINGULAR		PLURAL	
me (m')	(to) me	nous	(to) us
te (t')	(to) you (familiar)	vous	(to) you (also formal singular)
lui	(to) him, her	leur	(to) them

b. Uses

An indirect object pronoun replaces an indirect object noun and answers the questions to whom? for whom?

J'écris à mon ami.	*I write to my friend.*
Je *lui* écris.	*I write to him.*

NOTE: The verbs *obéir* (to obey), *désobéir* (to disobey), *répondre* (to answer), *ressembler* (to resemble), and *téléphoner* (to telephone) take an indirect object in French.

Elle téléphone *à ses parents*.	*She telephones her parents.*
Elle *leur* téléphone.	*She telephones them.*

c. Position

1. Indirect object pronouns normally precede the verb.

Elle *lui* répond.	*She answers him.*
Il *ne* lui téléphone pas.	*He doesn't call her.*
***Leur* obéit-il?**	*Does he obey them?*

EXERCISE F À l'université. You are away at college. Your mother wants to know if you are keeping in touch with your family. Express the conversation you have with her.

EXAMPLE: écrire à ton frère (oui)   annoncer tes nouvelles à ton père (non)
   Lui écris-tu?   **Lui annonces-tu tes nouvelles?**
   Je lui écris.   **Je ne lui annonce pas mes nouvelles.**

1. envoyer une carte à ta sœur (oui)

   _____

   _____

2. téléphoner à tes grands-parents (oui)

   _____

   _____

3. parler à ta nièce (non)

   _____

   _____

4. raconter des histoires à ton neveu (non)

_____

_____

5. demander des nouvelles à tes cousins (oui)

_____

_____

6. expliquer tes problèmes à ta tante et à ton oncle (non)

_____

_____

> **2.** When a pronoun is the indirect object of an infinitive, the pronoun precedes the infinitive.
>
> | | |
> |---|---|
> | **Je veux *vous* parler.** | *I want to speak to you.* |
> | **Vous ne voulez pas *me* parler.** | *You don't want to speak to me.* |
> | **Voulez-vous *lui* parler?** | *Do you want to speak to him?* |

EXERCISE G   **Des services.**   A friend asks if you can do things for him/her. For each of the following, write the question being asked and your negative or affirmative answer.

EXAMPLE: donner un conseil (oui)   enseigner les maths (non)
      Peux-tu me donner un conseil?   **Peux-tu m'enseigner les maths?**
      Je peux te donner un conseil.   **Je ne peux pas t'enseigner les maths.**

1. donner un coup de main (oui)

_____

_____

2. prêter cent dollars (non)

_____

_____

3. acheter un livre (oui)

_____

_____

4. offrir de l'aide financière (non)

_____

_____

5. rendre un service (oui)

_____

_____

6. apprendre à nager (non)

_____

_____

EXERCISE H   **La colère.**   These people are angry at their friends. Express what they don't
want to do, using the correct pronoun.

EXAMPLE: Janine veut dire ses secrets à Michelle.

Elle ne veut pas lui dire ses secrets.

1. Arnaud veut parler à Rémy.   _____

2. Maurice veut donner un cadeau à Lise.   _____

3. Bruno veut téléphoner à Irène.   _____

4. Céline veut écrire un mot à Jérôme.   _____

5. Charlotte veut raconter l'histoire à Josette et à Paul. _____

6. Carole veut expliquer le problème à ses amis.   _____

---

3. In an affirmative command, the indirect object pronoun follows the verb and is
attached to it by a hyphen. The pronouns *me* and *te* change to *moi* and *toi*. In a
negative command, the object pronoun retains its position before the verb.

AFFIRMATIVE COMMAND		NEGATIVE COMMAND	
Parle-lui!	*Speak to him!*	**Ne lui parle pas!**	*Don't speak to him!*
Écris-moi!	*Write to me!*	**Ne m'écris pas!**	*Don't write to me!*

EXERCISE I   **Une dispute.**   Juliette and Delphine had an argument. Their friend Béatrice
tells Juliette to do one thing while Géraldine advises her not to. Express
what Béatrice and Géraldine say.

EXAMPLE: donner un cadeau à Delphine

Donne-lui un cadeau.   **Ne lui donne pas** de cadeau.

1. parler à Delphine   _____

2. écrire une lettre à Delphine _____

3. dire à Delphine que tu l'aimes _____

4. montre ta sincérité à Delphine _____

5. répondre calmement à Delphine _____

6. téléphoner à Delphine _____

3.   The Pronoun *y*

The adverbial pronoun *y* always refers to previously mentioned things or places. It generally replaces *à* + noun but may also replace other prepositions of position or location such as *chez, dans, en, sous,* or *sur* + noun. The pronoun *y* most commonly means to it/them, in it/them, on it/them, and there. Sometimes the meaning of *y* is not expressed in English.

Il va *à Nice*.	*He is going to Nice.*
Il *y* va.	*He is going there.*
Elle répond *au message*.	*She answers the message.*
Elle *y* répond.	*She answers it.*
Ils sont *dans le tiroir*?	*Are they in the drawer?*
Oui, ils *y* sont.	*Yes, they are.*

NOTE: 1. The pronoun *y* follows the same rules of position in the sentence as direct and indirect object pronouns.

Y vont-ils?	*Are they going there?*
Il *y* va.	*He is going there.*
Elle n'*y* va pas.	*She isn't going there.*
Elle ne veut pas *y* aller.	*She doesn't want to go there.*

2. Affirmative familiar commands (*tu* form) of *–er* verbs and *aller* retain the final *s* before *y*.

AFFIRMATIVE COMMAND		NEGATIVE COMMAND	
Voyages-y!	*Travel there!*	**N'y voyage pas!**	*Don't travel there!*
Vas-y!	*Go there!*	**N'y va pas!**	*Don't go there.*

EXERCISE J **Les vacances.** People make statements, ask questions, and give their thoughts about vacation. Express their ideas by putting *y* in its proper place in the sentence.

1. Je vais chez moi. _____

2. Il ne va pas à St. Martin. _____

3. Tu ne peux pas voyager en Europe. _____

4. Nous ne voulons pas descendre en ville. _____

5. Vont-ils jouer au golf en France? _____

6. Dîne dans un bon restaurant!   _____

7. Ne pense pas au travail.   _____

8. Sont-elles maintenant en Afrique?   _____

4.   The Pronoun *en*

a. The adverbial pronoun *en* refers to previously mentioned nouns introduced by *de*. It means about it/them, from it/them, of it/them, or from there when it replaces a noun referring to places or things and introduced by the preposition *de*.

Je viens *de France*.	*I come from France.*
J'en viens.	*I come from there.*
Elle parle *de son examen.*	*She talks about her test.*
Elle e*n* parle.	*She talks about it.*

b. *En* means some or any (of it/them) when it replaces a noun introduced by the partitive article. In this case it may refer to persons as well as things.

Tu veux *du lait*?	*Do you want some milk?*
Oui, j'en veux.	*Yes, I want some.*
Tu prends *des fruits*?	*Are you taking any fruit?*
Non, je n'en prends pas.	*No, I'm not taking any.*
Tu as *des amis français*?	*Do you have any French friends?*
Oui, j'en ai.	*Yes, I have some.*

c. *En* is also used when the noun is omitted after a number or an expression of quantity.

Tu as *cent dollars*?	*Do you have a hundred dollars?*
Non, j'en ai soixante.	*No, I have sixty (of them).*
Tu as *des problèmes*?	*Do you have any problems?*
Oui, j'en ai beaucoup.	*Yes, I have a lot (of them).*

d. *En* is always expressed in French even though it may have no English equivalent.

Avez-vous *de l'argent*?	*Do you have money?*
Oui, j'en ai.	*Yes, I do.*

NOTE: 1.   *En* follows the same rules of position in the sentence as other object pronouns.

Je veux *en* **goûter.**	*I want to taste some.*
Il n'en veut pas.	*He doesn't want any.*
***En* veux-tu?**	*Do you want some?*
Je ne vais pas *en* **acheter.**	*I'm not going to buy any.*
Peux-tu *en* **prendre?**	*Can you take any of them?*

2. Affirmative familiar commands (*tu* form) of –*er* verbs retain the *s* before *en*.

Manges-en!	*Eat some!*
N'en mange pas!	*Don't eat any!*

3. *En* precedes *voici* and *voilà*.

En voilà (un).	*Here are some.* [*Here is one* (*of them*)].

EXERCISE K | **De la glace.** Everyone has his or her favorite ice cream flavor. Rewrite the story by substituting *en* for the underlined words.

Je sors de mon appartement. J'ai dix dollars. Je veux manger de la glace. Je ne veux jamais prendre de glace au chocolat. Je demande au propriétaire, "Avez-vous de la glace à la vanille?" Il répond, "N'achète pas de vanille. Eh bien, nous n'avons pas de vanille. Prends du chocolat. C'est vraiment délicieux! Alors, vas-tu prendre du chocolat?" Alors, rien à faire. J'achète deux glaces au chocolat.

_____

_____

_____

_____

5. Relative Pronouns

A relative pronoun introduces a clause that describes someone or something mentioned in the main clause. The person or thing the pronoun refers to is called the antecedent because it precedes the relative pronoun. The most common relative pronouns are *qui* and *que*.

a. *Qui*

Qui (who, which, that) serves as the subject of the verb in the relative clause that it introduces. It is used for both person and things.

[relative clause]
Voici **un *professeur* qui adore** ses étudiants.
[*antecedent*] [subject]   [verb]

Here is a teacher who loves his students.

[relative clause]
La Jaguar est **une *voiture* qui est** vraiment belle.
[*antecedent*] [subject] [verb]

The Jaguar is a car that is really beautiful.

NOTE: The verb of a relative clause introduced by *qui* agrees with its antecedent noun or stress pronoun.

[relative clause]
C'est **moi qui fais** tout.
[*antecedent*] [subject] [verb]

I do everything.

EXERCISE L   **Les préférences.**   Express the preferences of these people by combining the sentences with the pronoun *qui*.

EXAMPLE: Elles cherchent un film. Il est amusant.
           Elles cherchent un film *qui* est amusant.

1. J'adore les voitures. Elle roulent vite.

   _____

2. Elle préfère un hôtel. Il donne sur la mer.

   _____

3. Nous aimons les vacances. Elle durent longtemps.

   _____

4. Ils choisissent des vêtements. Ils sont à la mode.

   _____

5. Tu détestes une histoire. Elle est triste.

   _____

6. Vous renoncez à des restaurants. Ils servent de la viande.

   _____

b. *Que*

Que (whom, which, that) serves as the direct object of the verb in a relative clause and is usually followed by a subject noun or pronoun. It is used for both persons and things. The relative pronoun is always expressed in French although it is frequently omitted in English. Note that *que* becomes *qu'* before a vowel.

[relative clause]
C'est **le professeur que je respecte** le plus   *That's the teacher (that)*
  [*antecedent*] [object] [subject] [verb]   *I respect the most.*

[relative clause]
Voilà **la voiture qu'elle veut.**   *There's the car (that) she wants.*
  [*antecedent*] [object] [subject] [verb]

EXERCISE M   **Les opinions.**   Complete the sentence by giving the opinion of each person.

EXAMPLE: (elle)   *La Vie en Rose* est une chanson **qu'elle chante drôlement bien.**

1. (je)   Le basket est un sport _____ .

2. (ils)   Le président est un homme _____ .

3. (nous)   Noël est une fête _____ .

4. (elle)   Sa mère est une personne _____ .

5. (tu)   La France est un pays _____ .

6. (vous)   La bouillabaisse est une soupe _____ .

| **EXERCISE N** | **Les voilà.**   Complete the sentences about these people who help others using *qui* or *que*. |

1. Voilà une dame _____ j'estime. C'est une dame _____ combat l'injustice.

2. Voilà un homme _____ guérit les malades. C'est un homme _____ nous aimons.

3. Voilà des gens _____ protègent l'environnement. Ce sont des gens _____ nous respectons.

4. Voilà des femmes _____ j'aime. Ce sont des femmes _____ aident les pauvres.

6.   Stress Pronouns

a. Forms

SINGULAR			PLURAL		
(je)	moi	*I, me*	(nous)	nous	*we*
(tu)	toi	*you* (familiar)	(vous)	vous	*you*
(il)	lui	*he, him*	(ils)	eux	*they, them*
(elle)	elle	*she, her*	(elles)	elles	*they, them*

b. Uses

A stress pronoun can function either as a subject or an object. It can either replace another word or reinforce it for added emphasis.

1.   Stress pronouns are used when no verb is expressed.

Qui est là? *Moi.*	*Who's there? —Me. (I am.)*
J'adore cette musique. *Elle aussi.*	*I love this music. So does she.*
Il est plus fort *que moi.*	*He is stronger than I.*

2.   Stress pronouns are used to add emphasis to a noun or another pronoun.

Moi, **je chante bien.**	*I sing well.*
Jean, *lui,* **arrive toujours tôt.**	*John always arrives early.*
Il l'aime bien, *elle.*	*He really likes her.*

3.   Stress pronouns are used after *ce + être*. Before *eux* and *elles* the verb *être* may be used either in the singular (*c'est eux, c'est elles*) or in the plural (*ce sont eux, ce sont elles*) although the singular is more commonly used.

| *C'est elles qui* **font tout le travail.** | *They are doing all the work.* |

4.   Stress pronouns are used after a preposition to refer to people.

| **Je vais** *chez lui.* | *I'm going to his house.* |

5. Stress pronouns are used in a compound subject or object. If one of the stress pronouns is *moi,* the verb is put in the first person plural and the *nous* may or may not be expressed. If *toi* is one of the stress pronouns, the verb is put in the second person plural (*vous* form).

Marthe et lui travaillent **ensemble.**	*Martha and he work together.*
Elle et moi **(, *nous*) sommes amies.**	*She and I are friends.*
Roger et toi **(, *vous*) dansez bien.**	*Roger and you dance well.*

EXERCISE O   **La fête.**   You and your friends are preparing for a party. Express what everyone does.

EXAMPLE: (elle)/aller en ville   **C'est elle qui va en ville.**

1. (il)/choisir la musique   _____.

2. (nous)/nettoyer la maison   _____

3. (tu)/acheter les provisions   _____

4. (elles)/cuisiner les plats   _____

5. (je)/préparer les sandwiches   _____

6. (elle)/écrire les invitations   _____

7. (vous)/faire les desserts   _____

8. (ils)/mettre la table   _____

EXERCISE P   **Actions réciproques.**   Express the reciprocal action.

EXAMPLE: Je reste chez toi.   **Tu restes chez moi.**

1. Il habite près de chez toi.   _____

2. Vous parlez de moi.   _____

3. Nous sommes assis devant eux.   _____

4. Elles jouent contre vous.   _____

5. Je travaille à côté de lui.   _____

6. Ils voyagent avec nous.   _____

EXERCISE Q   **Les amusements.**   Work with a partner. Take turns asking each other about three things you like and dislike.

EXAMPLE: Les films d'horreur. Tu les aimes?
   Oui, je les aime.
   Non, je ne les aime pas.

_____

_____

_____

_____

_____

_____

EXERCISE R   Write a letter to your cousins thanking them for a gift they gave you. Explain
why you like it and what you will do with it.

_____

_____

_____

_____

_____

Chapter 12
Prepositions

Prepositions relate two elements of a sentence (noun to noun; verb to noun, pronoun, or another verb). The most frequently used prepositions in French are *à* and *de*.

C'est la voiture *de* nos parents.	*It's our parents' car.*
Je vais *à* la campagne.	*I'm going to the country.*
Elle sort *avec* ses amies.	*She's going out with her friends.*

1. Common Prepositions

à* *at, in, to*
après *after*
autour de *around*
avant (de) *before*
avec *with*
chez (+ person) *to, at (the house/place of a person)*
contre *against*
dans *in, into, within*
de† *about, from, of*
derrière *behind*
devant *in front of*
en *at; by; in*
entre *between, among*
loin de *far from*
par *by, through*
près de *near*
sans *without*
sur *on, upon*
vers *towards*

EXERCISE A Une invitation. Complete the story about the two boys by using the appropriate preposition.

à	avec	dans	du
après	chez	derrière	loin

---

* *à* contracts with *le* to become *au* and with *les* to become *aux*.
† *De* contracts with *le* to become *du* and with *les* to become *des*.

Serge travaille ————— son jardin qui est situé ————— sa maison. ————— une heure il
1.   2.   3.

est fatigué et il décide de téléphoner ————— son ami Xavier. Ils parlent ————— week-
4.   5.

end. Serge invite Xavier ————— lui. Il va venir ————— un autre camarade de classe qui
6.   7.

n'habite pas ————— des deux garçons.
8.

2.   Prepositions Used Before an Infinitive

In French, the infinitive is the verb form that normally follows a preposition.

a. Some verbs require *à* before an infinitive.

s'amuser*à   *to have fun*
commencer à   *to begin to*
continuer à   *to continue to*
demander à   *to ask to*
encourager à   *to encourage to*
se mettre*à   *to begin to*
penser à   *to think about*
se préparer*à   *to prepare to*
renoncer à   *to give up*
réussir à   *to succeed in*

Il continue *à conduire* vite.   *He continues driving quickly.*

b. Some verbs require *de* before an infinitive.

s'arrêter*de   *to stop*
choisir de   *to choose to*
décider de   *to decide to*
se dépêcher*de   *to hurry to*
essayer de   *to try to*
oublier de   *to forget to*
parler de   *to speak about*
refuser de   *to refuse to*
regretter de   *to regret to*
rêver de   *to dream about*

Elle s'arrête *de parler*.   *She stops speaking.*

---

* For more information on reflexive verbs, see Chapter 16.

| **EXERCISE B** | **Le rendez-vous.** Baptiste has a date with Monique. Complete the story with the appropriate preposition. |

Baptiste a un rendez-vous à un café avec Monique et il regrette _____ avoir l'habitude
1.

de toujours arriver en retard. Cette fois-ci il refuse _____ être le dernier à arriver
2.

au café à quatre heures. Il se prépare _____ y aller et il renonce absolument
3.

_____ être en retard. Avant de partir il choisit _____ s'amuser _____
4.   5.   6.

jouer aux jeux vidéo. Il s'arrête _____ jouer trop tard et il se dépêche _____
7.   8.

partir. Oh là là, en quittant sa maison il oublie _____ fermer la porte et il doit rentrer.
9.

Il commence _____ devenir nerveux et il essaie _____ aller plus rapidement.
10.   11.

Il continue _____ marcher très vite. Puis, finalement, il se met _____ courir
12.   13.

encore plus rapidement quand il pense _____ Monique qui va sûrement être très
14.

fâchée. Il est tout près du café quand il regarde sa montre. Il pousse un soupir de soulage-

ment quand il est sûr qu'il va réussir _____ arriver avant Monique. Pourquoi est-il si
15.

sûr? Sa montre avance et il est trois heures moins cinq au lieu de quatre heures moins cinq.

c. Some other prepositions are commonly followed by an infinitive.

au lieu de *instead of*
avant de *before*
pour *in order to, for the purpose of*
sans *without*

Il parle *sans réfléchir*.   *He speaks without thinking.*

| **EXERCISE C** | **Les circonstances.** Complete the sentences about yourself stating what you do under these circumstances. |

agir	étudier	avoir de bonnes notes
penser	sortir	demander la permission
	travailler	regarder la télé

EXAMPLE: Quand je suis furieux (furieuse) je **pleure** au lieu de **crier.**

1. Quand je suis fatigué(e) je _____ au lieu de _____ .

2. Quand je suis nerveux (nerveuse) je _____ sans _____ .

3. Quand je suis diligent(e) je —————— pour ———————————— .

4. Quand je suis prudent(e) je ———————————— avant de —————— .

d. Some verbs are followed by an infinitive without a preposition.

aimer   *to like, love*
aller   *to go*
compter   *to intend*
désirer   *to wish, want*
espérer   *to hope*
penser   *to intend*
pouvoir   *to be able*
préférer   *to prefer*
savoir   *to know how to*
vouloir   *to wish, want*

Je sais nager.	*I know how to swim.*
Nous ne pouvons pas venir.	*We can't come.*
Préfèrent-ils jouer au basket?	*Do they prefer to play basketball?*

EXERCISE D   **Les intentions.**   Express what each person intends to do today.

EXAMPLE: ils/désirer
Ils **désirent jouer** avec l'ordinateur.

1. je/compter ————————————

———————————— .

2. elles/aimer ————————————

———————————— .

3. nous/préférer _____

_____ .

4. il/espérer _____

_____ .

5. vous/vouloir _____

_____ .

6. tu/penser _____

_____ .

3.   Prepositions with Geographical Expressions

The prepositions *à* (in, to), *en* (in, to), and *de* (*d'*) show location.

LOCATION	IN	TO	FROM
Cities	à	à	de (d')
Feminine countries, continents, provinces, and islands and masculine countries that begin with a vowel	en	en	de (d')
All other masculine countries	au	au	du
All plurals	aux	aux	des

NOTE: 1. Geographical names are feminine if they end in *–e* with the exception of *le Mexique, le Cambodge* (Cambodia) and *le Zaïre.*

2. The definite article is not used with Israël and Haïti.

3. Feminine countries, continents, provinces.

l'Allemagne	*Germany*	**la Chine**	*China*
l'Angleterre	*England*	**l'Écosse**	*Scotland*
l'Autriche	*Austria*	**l'Égypte**	*Egypt*
la Belgique	*Belgium*	**l'Espagne**	*Spain*

la France	*France*	**la Norvège**	*Norway*
la Grèce	*Greece*	**la Pologne**	*Poland*
Haïti	*Haiti*	**la Roumanie**	*Romania*
la Hongrie	*Hungary*	**la Russie**	*Russia*
l'Irlande	*Ireland*	**la Suède**	*Sweden*
l'Italie	*Italy*	**la Suisse**	*Switzerland*

l'Afrique	*Africa*
l'Amérique du Nord	*North America*
l'Amérique du Sud	*South America*
l'Asie	*Asia*
l'Australie	*Australia*
l'Europe	*Europe*

l'Alsace	*Alsace*	**la Flandre**	*Flanders*
la Bourgogne	*Burgundy*	**la Lorraine**	*Lorraine*
la Bretagne	*Brittany*	**la Normandie**	*Normandy*
la Champagne	*Champagne*	**la Provence**	*Provence*

4. Masculine countries

le Brésil	*Brazil*
le Canada	*Canada*
le Cambodge	*Cambodia*
le Danemark	*Denmark*
les États-Unis	*the United States*
Israël	*Israel*
le Japon	*Japan*
le Maroc	*Morocco*
le Mexique	*Mexico*
les Pays-Bas	*the Netherlands, Holland*
le Portugal	*Portugal*
le Zaïre	*Zaire*

5. Mountains and waterways follow the rules for countries; they are usually feminine if they end in *-e.*

les Alpes (f.)	*the Alps*
le Jura	*the Jura Mountains*
les Pyrénées (f.)	*the Pyrenees*
les Vosges (f.)	*the Vosges*
la Manche	*the English Channel*
la mer Méditerranée	*the Mediterranean Sea*
la Loire	*the Loire*

le Rhin	*the Rhine*
la Seine	*the Seine*
le Rhône	*the Rhone*
la Garonne	*the Garonne*

EXERCISE E   **Le va-et-vient.** Tell where these people are coming from and where they are going.

EXAMPLE: il/Allemagne/Grèce   Il vient **d'Allemagne** et il va **en Grèce.**

1. je/Canada/États-Unis _____

2. vous/Maroc/Égypte _____

3. ils/Mexique/Espagne _____

4. nous/Pays-Bas/Japon _____

5. elle/Angleterre/Italie _____

6. tu/Haïti/France _____

4.   Expressions Introduced by *à*

1. Mode of travel

à bicyclette	*on, by bicycle*
à cheval	*on horseback*
à pied	*on foot*

2. Time

à bientôt	*see you soon, so long*
à ce soir	*see you tonight*
à demain	*see you tomorrow*
à samedi	*see you Saturday*
à l'heure	*on time*
à tout à l'heure	*see you later*
au revoir	*good-bye, see you again*

3. Position and direction

à côté (de)	*next to, beside*
à droite (de)	*on (to) the right (of)*
à gauche (de)	*on (to) the left (of)*
au bas de	*at the bottom of*
au fond (de)	*in (at) the bottom (of)*
au haut (de)	*in (at) the top (of))*
au milieu (de)	*in the middle (of)*

4. Other expressions

à la campagne	*in (to) the country*
à la maison	*at home, home*
à l'école	*in (to) school*
à peu près	*nearly, about, approximately*
à voix haute, à haute voix	*aloud, out loud, in a loud voice*
à voix basse	*in a low voice*
au contraire	*on the contrary*
au moins	*at least*

EXERCISE F   **Ma maison.**   Complete the story by adding the correct expression.

à bicyclette   à la campagne
à côté   à peu près
à l'heure   au contraire

Ma maison n'est pas petite. ——————— , elle est grande. Nous n'aimons pas la ville. Là il

         1.

y a trop de bruit. Nous préférons la tranquillité, alors nous habitons ——————— . Il y a un

         2.

jardin et un lac ——————— de ma maison.   J'habite assez loin de l'école, qui est

      3.

——————— à six kilomètres de chez moi. J'y vais ——————— et j'y arrive toujours

  4.   5.

——————— .

  6.

5. Expressions Introduced by *de, en,* and *par*

d'abord	*first, at first*
d'accord	*agreed, O.K.*
de bonne heure	*early*
de l'autre côté (de)	*on the other side (of)*
de quelle couleur..?	*What color?*
de rien. **il n'y a pas de quoi.** }	*You're welcome. Don't mention it.*
de temps en temps	*from time to time*
en	*by (when one is inside the means of transportation)*
en avion	*by plane*
en voiture	*by car*
en	*in (with the name of a language)*
en bas	*downstairs,* (**en bas de** *at the bottom of*)
en haut	*upstairs,* (**en haut de** *at the top of*)
en face (de)	*opposite*

en avance	*early*
en retard	*late, not on time*
en ville	*downtown, in (to, into) town*

par exemple	*for example*
par jour (semaine, mois, etc.)	*a/per day (week, month, etc.)*

EXERCISE G   **Les expressions.**   Choose an expression above that best completes the sentence.

1. On va en Europe —————————— .

2. On mange trois fois —————————— .

3. Si on n'arrive pas à l'heure, on est —————————— .

4. Si on arrive avant l'heure indiquée, on arrive —————————— .

5. Si on dîne assez souvent au restaurant, on y dîne —————————— .

6. Les livres de Jean-Paul Sartre sont écrits —————————— .

7. Si une personne dit "merci" l'autre personne répond, —————————— .

8. Si nous avons la même opinion sur un sujet, nous sommes —————————— .

EXERCISE H   **Où sont les magasins?**   Read the directions and then indicate where the different buildings are located.

le théâtre Jules Romain	la pharmacie Optima
le musée d'art moderne	la boulangerie Lévêque
le cinéma Rex	l'épicerie Botard
le restaurant Chez Jacques	

À gauche du café il y a le théâtre Jules Romain. À droite du café il y a le musée d'art moderne.
Et à côté du musée il y a la pharmacie Optima. De l'autre côté de la rue, en face de la pharmacie, il y a le restaurant Chez Jacques et en face du café il y a le cinéma Rex. Entre le cinéma et
la pharmacie se trouve la boulangerie Lévêque. Et à gauche du cinéma et tout droit devant le
théatre se trouve l'épicerie Botard.

EXERCISE I   **Allons à l'école.**   Work with a partner. Take turns discussing where your
house is located and how you get to school.

_____

_____

_____

_____

EXERCISE J   **Les rêves.**   Write a paragraph that begins, "Je rêve de…" in which you
express your dreams about what you want to accomplish in the future and
how you intend to realize your dreams.

_____

_____

_____

_____

CHAPTER 13
Possession

1. Expressing Possession

a. The preposition *de* (*d'*) expresses possession and relationship in French and is the equivalent of the English *'s* or *s'* (of). *De* must be repeated before each noun. *De* contracts with *le* to become *du* and with *les* to become *des*.

Ce sont les parents *d'*Éric et *de* Michel.	*They are Eric's and Michel's parents.*
Voilà le cartable *du* garçon.	*There is the boy's bookbag.*
Il lit les poèmes *des* étudiants.	*He reads the students' poems.*

EXERCISE A   **Les résultats.**   Express what belongs to each person.

EXAMPLES: la sculpture/le sculpteur   C'est la sculpture **du** sculpteur.

les CD/la musicienne   Ce sont les CD **de** la musicienne.

1. la peinture/l'artiste _____

2. les édifices/les architectes _____

3. le gâteau/le pâtissier _____

4. les plats/le chef _____

5. les lettres/les secrétaires _____

6. les documents/l'avocat _____

7. les pains/la boulangère _____

8. les légumes/le fermier _____

b. The idiom *être à* (to belong to) also expresses possession. *À* must be repeated before each noun. *À* contracts with *le* to become *au* and with *les* to become *aux*.

Ces livres *sont à* Robert et *à* moi.	*These are Robert's and my books.*
Ce vélo est *au* garçon.	*This bicycle is the boy's.*
Ces stylos sont *aux* élèves.	*These pens are the students'.*

EXERCISE B   **La lessive.**   Your father has just done the laundry and doesn't know which clothing belongs to whom. Help him.

EXAMPLE: ta sœur
PAPA: Cette robe est à ta sœur?
VOUS: Oui, **c'est à elle.**

1. toi

_____

_____

2. Patrick

_____

_____

3. ton frère et toi

_____

_____

4. Louise et Paul

_____

_____

5. maman

_____

_____

6. moi

_____

_____

2. Possessive Adjectives

SINGULAR		PLURAL	MEANING
MASCULINE	FEMININE		
mon	ma	mes	*my*
ton	ta	tes	*your* (familiar)
son	sa	ses	*his, her, its*
notre	notre	nos	*our*
votre	votre	vos	*your* (formal or plural)
leur	leur	leurs	*their*

NOTE: 1. Possessive adjectives, like other adjectives, agree in number and gender with the nouns they modify. They are repeated before each noun.

Il aime *sa* mère et *son* père.   *He loves his mother and his father.*

J'aime *sa* sœur.   *I love his (her) sister.*

2. The forms *mon, ton,* and *son* are used instead of *ma, ta,* and *sa* before a feminine singular noun beginning with a vowel or silent *h*.

Janine est *mon* amie.   *Janine is my friend.*

Mange *ton* omelette!   *Eat your omelet!*

Il parle à *son* avocate.   *He speaks to his (female) lawyer.*

3. With parts of the body, the possessive adjective is usually replaced by the definite article if the possessor is clear.

Il se lave *la* figure.   *He washes his face.*

EXERCISE C   **Le retard.**   Students may sometimes be late for school because they can't find something they'll need during the day. Express what each person is looking for.

EXAMPLE: il/livre   Il cherche **son** livre.

1. tu/blouson   _____

2. elle/sac à dos   _____

3. vous/stylos   _____

4. ils/cahiers   _____

5. je/calculette   _____

6. nous/parapluie   _____

7. elles/dictionnaire   _____

8. il/règle   _____

EXERCISE D   **Les dialogues.**   Answer the question at the end of each dialogue with a possessive adjective.

EXAMPLE: J'ai un livre. Je vais le donner à Claudine.
Qu'est-ce que tu vas donner à Claudine?
Mon livre.

1. Roger a une petite amie. Il l'adore.
Qui est-ce qu'il adore?

_____

2. Jean et François ont des chiens. Ils les amènent toujours au café.
Qui est-ce qu'ils amènent au café?

_____

3. Les Pascal ont une nouvelle voiture de sport. Ils la conduisent partout.
Qu'est-ce qu'ils conduisent partout?

_____

4. Martine a de nouveaux CD. Elle va les écouter quand elle arrive à la maison.
Qu'est-ce qu'elle va écouter?

_____

5. Carine a un grand problème. Elle va le discuter avec sa meilleure amie.
Qu'est-ce qu'elle va discuter?

_____

6. Les Jeannot ont une maison. Ils veulent la peindre.
Qu'est-ce qu'ils veulent peindre?

_____

EXERCISE E   Work with a partner. Take turns asking and answering the personal questions below. Then write your responses and those of your partner.

1. Quel est ton nom?

_____

_____

2. Quelle est ton adresse?

_____

_____

3. Quel est ton numéro de téléphone?

_____

_____

4. Qui est ton (ta) meilleur(e) ami(e)?

_____

_____

5. Quelles sont tes émissions de télévision préférées?

_____

_____

6. Qui est ton acteur préféré?

_____

_____

7. Qui est ton actrice préférée?

_____

_____

8. Quel est ton plat préféré?

_____

_____

EXERCISE F Write a letter to your friend about the people in your family. Give their names, ages, and professions.

_____

_____

_____

_____

_____

_____

CHAPTER 14
Adjectives

An adjective is a word that describes a noun or pronoun.

La maison est *blanche.*   *The house is white.*

1. Agreement of Adjectives

French adjectives agree in gender (masculine or feminine) and in number (singular or plural) with the nouns or pronouns they modify.

Le garçon est *grand* **et la fille est** *petite.*   *The boy is big and the girl is little.*

a. Gender of Adjectives

1. Most adjectives, including those ending in *é*, form the feminine by adding *e* to the masculine.

MASCULINE	FEMININE	
bleu	bleue	*blue*
content	contente	*happy*
fatigué	fatiguée	*tired*
joli	jolie	*pretty*
lourd	lourde	*heavy*

2. Adjectives ending in silent –*e* do not change in the feminine.

Le monument est célèbre.   *The monument is famous.*
La cathédrale est *célèbre.*   *The cathedral is famous.*

EXERCISE A   **Ma maison.**   Complete the sentences to describe your house, choosing appropriate adjectives.

grand	petit	confortable
moderne	joli	splendide

1. Ma maison est —————————— .

2. Mon jardin est —————————— .

3. Ma cuisine est —————————— .

4. Mon garage est —————————— .

5. Mon living est —————————— .

6. Ma chambre est —————————— .

3. Adjectives ending in *–x* form the feminine by changing *–x* to *–se*.

Le garçon est sérieux.	*The boy is serious.*
La fille est sérieuse.	*The girl is serious.*

4. Adjectives ending in *–f* form the feminine by changing *–f* to *–ve*.

Jean est actif.	*Jean is active.*
Jeanne est active.	*Jeanne is active.*

5. Adjectives ending in *–er* form the feminine by changing *–er* to *–ère*.

Le scooter est cher.	*The scooter is expensive.*
La voiture est chère.	*The car is expensive.*

6. Some adjectives double the final consonant before adding *–e* in the feminine.

MASCULINE	FEMININE	
ancien	**ancienne**	*old, ancient, former*
bas	**basse**	*low*
bon	**bonne**	*good*
cruel	**cruelle**	*cruel*
européen	**européenne**	*European*
gentil	**gentille**	*nice, kind*
gros	**grosse**	*fat*

7. Some adjectives have irregular feminine forms.

MASCULINE	FEMININE	
blanc	**blanche**	*white*
complet	**complète**	*complete*
doux	**douce**	*sweet, mild, gentle*
faux	**fausse**	*false*
favori	**favorite**	*favorite*
frais	**fraîche**	*fresh, cool*
franc	**franche**	*frank*
long	**longue**	*long*
secret	**secrète**	*secret*
beau (bel)	**belle**	*beautiful*
nouveau (nouvel)	**nouvelle**	*new*
vieux (vieil)	**vieille**	*old*

NOTE: The adjectives *beau, nouveau,* and *vieux* change to *bel, nouvel,* and *vieil* before a masculine singular noun beginning with a vowel or silent *h*.

Cet appartement est beau (nouveau) (vieux).	*This apartment is beautiful (new) (old).*
C'est un *bel* (nouvel) (vieil) appartement.	*It's a beautiful (new) (old) apartment.*

EXERCISE B   **Les connaissances.** Describe these people you know.

1. (honnête)   Constance est ——————————— .

2. (content)   Guy est ——————————— .

3. (grand)   Florence est ——————————— .

4. (joli)   Cassandre est ——————————— .

5. (aimable)   Sylvain est ——————————— .

6. (méchant)   Géraldine est ——————————— .

7. (populaire) Didier est ——————————— .

8. (bon)   Fernande est ——————————— .

9. (cruel)   Gabrielle est ——————————— .

10. (gentil)   Vincent est ——————————— .

11. (doux)   Janine est ——————————— .

12. (franc)   Henriette est ——————————— .

EXERCISE C   **Les gens.** Describe these people by selecting the appropriate adjective and putting it in its proper form.

cruel   impulsif   superstitieux
gros   paresseux   vieux
heureux   sportif

1. Mme Renard a plus de cent ans. Elle est vraiment ——————————— .

2. Jean et Arnaud mangent beaucoup et ils pèsent plus de 125 kilos. Ils sont vraiment

——————————— .

3. Yvette aime tous les sports. Elle est vraiment ——————————— .

4. Robert croit que le numéro treize porte malheur. Il est vraiment ——————————— .

5. Alice ne fait jamais ses devoirs. Elle est vraiment ——————————— .

6. Anne sourit toujours et elle est toujours contente. Elle est vraiment

——————————— .

7. Mariane est très méchante. Elle dit des mensonges et elle ridiculise les gens. Elle est

vraiment ——————————— .

8. Damien parle et agit sans réfléchir. Il est vraiment ——————————— .

EXERCISE D   **Le logement.**   Describe the places to live by completing each sentence with the correct form of the adjective in parentheses.

1. (beau) Ce _____ appartement a une _____ cuisine, une _____

   entrée et un _____ salon.

2. (vieux) Mon _____ grand-père habite un _____ immeuble dans un

   _____ quartier d'une _____ ville.

3. (nouveau) Je cherche une _____ maison près d'une _____ église, un

   _____ supermarché et un _____ hôpital.

b. Plural of Adjectives

1. The plural of most adjectives is formed by adding –s to the singular whether masculine or feminine.

MASCULINE		FEMININE		MEANING
SINGULAR	PLURAL	SINGULAR	PLURAL	
bleu	bleus	bleue	bleues	blue
content	contents	contente	contentes	happy
fatigué	fatigués	fatiguée	fatiguées	tired
joli	jolis	jolie	jolies	pretty
bon	bons	bonne	bonnes	good
sportif	sportifs	sportive	sportives	sporty
gentil	gentils	gentille	gentilles	nice, kind

2. Adjectives ending in –s or –x do not change in the masculine plural.

   Cet homme est anglais.   *That man is English.*
   Ces hommes sont *anglais*.   *Those men are English.*

   Il est heureux.   *He is happy.*
   Ils sont *heureux*.   *They are happy.*

3. Most adjectives ending in –al change –al to –aux in the masculine plural.

   Ce livre est spécial.   *This book is special.*
   Ces livres sont spéciaux.   *These books are special.*

4. The singular masculine adjective *tout* is irregular and becomes *tous* in the masculine plural.

   ***Tous* les garçons sont là.**   *All the boys are there.*

5. Both masculine forms of *beau* (*bel*), *nouveau* (*nouvel*) and *vieux* (*vieil*) have the same plural forms.

   un beau (nouveau) (vieux) théâtre   *a beautiful (new) (old) theater*
   de *beaux* (*nouveaux*) (*vieux*) théâtres   *beautiful (new) (old) theaters*

un bel (nouvel) (vieil) hôtel   *a beautiful (new) (old) hotel*
de *beaux* (*nouveaux*) (*vieux*) hôtels   *beautiful (new) (old) hotels*

NOTE: 1.   When an adjective precedes a plural noun, *des* becomes *de.*

de jolies maisons   *pretty houses*

2.   An adjective modifying two or more nouns of different genders is masculine plural.

L'appartement et la maison sont *jolis.*   *The appartment and the house are pretty.*

EXERCISE E   **Les contraires.**   Rewrite each sentence giving the adjective that expresses the opposite.

1. Les montagnes sont hautes. _____

2. Les routes sont courtes. _____

3. Les maisons sont noires. _____

4. Les avenues sont larges. _____

5. Les chemins sont mauvais. _____

6. Les édifices sont laids. _____

EXERCISE F   **Au supermarché.**   Give your opinion of the foods you see by using the plural of the adjectives.

1. La pomme est spéciale et les raisins sont _____ .

2. Le fruit est frais et les cerises sont _____ .

3. Le brocoli est mauvais et les carottes sont _____ .

4. Le gâteau est cher et les tartes sont _____ .

5. Le potage est délicieux et les soupes sont _____ .

6. La prune est belle et les melons sont _____ .

2.   Position of Adjectives

a. Descriptive adjectives normally follow the noun they modify.

un chat noir   *a black cat*

b. Some short descriptive adjectives usually precede the noun.

beau
bon/mauvais
court/long

> **gentil**
> **gros**
> **jeune/vieux**
> **joli**
> **nouveau**
> **petit/grand**

un vieux monsieur   *an old gentleman*

> **NOTE:** Remember that *des* becomes *de* when a plural adjective precedes a plural noun.
>
> **de longues histoires**   *long stories*

c. Some other common adjectives precede the noun.

> **autre** *other*
> **chaque** *each*
> **dernier** *last*
> **plusieurs** (*m./f. pl.*) *several*
> **premier** *first*
> **quelques** (*m./f. pl.*) *a few*
> **tel** *such*

une autre raison   *another reason*

d. The adjective *tout* (all, whole, every) precedes both the noun and the definite article.

> **tout le monde** *everybody*
> **toute la journée** *all day*
> **tous les jours** *every day*
> **toutes les femmes** *every woman*

| **EXERCISE G** | **Une promenade.** Describe what each person sees by giving the correct form of the adjective and by putting it in its proper place. |

EXAMPLES: (vert) il/de l'herbe   Il voit de l'herbe **verte.**
(grand) on/plantes   On voit de **grandes** plantes.

1. (magnifique) nous/un paysage _____

2. (gris) ils/un ciel _____

3. (long) vous/une rivière _____

4. (vieux) elle/des arbres _____

5. (étroit) je/des rues _____

6. (joli) tu/fleurs _____

7. (beau)   il/des lacs   _____

8. (brillant) elles/une lune _____

3.   Comparison of Adjectives

Things or people can be compared with each other by using the comparative or superlative of the adjectives that modify them. Comparisons are formed as follows.

plus (*more*)
moins (*less*)   } + adjective + **que**
aussi (*as*)

La pièce est *plus* (*moins*) (*aussi*)   *The play is more (less) (as)*
  intéressante que le film.   *interesting (than) (as) the film.*

The superlative is formed as follows.

le (la, les) plus (*the most*)
le (la, les) moins (*the least*) } + adjective + **de**

Georgette est *la plus* (*moins*)   *Georgette is the most (least)*
  belle des filles.   *beautiful of the girls.*

Ces hommes sont *les moins* optimistes.   *These men are the least optimistic.*

NOTE: The adjective *bon* (good) has an irregular comparative *meilleur* (better) and superlative *le meilleur* (the best). The comparative and superlative of the adjective *mauvais* (bad) are *pire* (worse) and *le pire* (the worst).

La vanille est *bonne* mais le   *Vanilla is good but chocolate is better.*
  chocolat est *meilleur.*

La chaleur est *mauvaise* mais   *Heat is bad but cold is worse.*
  le froid est *pire.*

EXERCISE H **Les comparaisons.** Give the opinions of people you know by making comparisons.

EXAMPLE: le vice-président/–/important/le président
     Le vice-président **est moins** important **que** le président.

1. la natation/–/dangereux/le hockey

_____

2. la cathédrale Notre-Dame/=/beau/le Sacré-Cœur

_____

3. les girafes/+/grand/les éléphants

_____

4. les écoles américaines/=/compréhensif/les écoles françaises

_____

5. les océans/+/long/les rivières

_____

6. le bateau/−/rapide/l'avion

_____

| EXERCISE I | **Mes amis.**   Tell people about your friends. |

EXAMPLES: Louise/−/ambitieux   Louise est **la moins** ambitieuse **de** mes amis.
            Joseph et Philippe/+/sympathique   Joseph et Philippe sont **les plus**
                                                                          sympathiques **de** mes amis.

1. Patrick/+/honnête   _____

2. Alice/−/imaginatif   _____

3. Roger et Bernard/−/loyal _____

4. Lise et Sylvie/+/sportif   _____

| EXERCISE J | **Les profs.**   Work with a partner. Take turns comparing four teachers in your school. |

_____

_____

_____

_____

_____

| EXERCISE K | **Comparaison.**   Write a letter to a friend comparing yourself to another family member. |

_____

_____

_____

_____

_____

CHAPTER 15
Adverbs

An adverb is a word that modifies a verb, an adjective or another adverb.

Il court *vite.*   *He runs quickly.*
Ce livre est *très* **intéressant.**   *This book is very interesting.*
Elle parle *assez lentement.*   *She speaks rather slowly.*

1.   Formation of Adverbs

Most French adverbs are formed by adding *–ment* to adjectives while most English adverbs are formed by adding *–ly* to adjectives.

a. When a masculine singular adjective ends in a vowel, *-ment* is added to the masculine singular form.

brave	*brave*	**bravement**	*bravely*
vrai	*true*	**vraiment**	*truly*

| EXERCISE A | **La maladie.** Your friend Arnaud is not feeling well. Combine the sentences to express his behavior. |

EXAMPLE: Il respire. Il est faible.

Il respire **faiblement.**

1. Il se fatigue. Il est rapide. _____

2. Il continue. Il est difficile. _____

3. Il parle. Il est triste. _____

4. Il travaille. Il est brave. _____

5. Il répond. Il est calme. _____

6. Il tousse. Il est facile. _____

b. When a masculine singular adjective ends in a consonant, *-ment* is added to the feminine singular form.

ADJECTIVE		ADVERB	
MASCULINE	FEMININE		
attentif	attentive	attentivement	*attentively*
certain	certaine	certainement	*certainly*
complet	complète	complètement	*completely*
cruel	cruelle	cruellement	*cruelly*
doux	douce	doucement	*softly, gently*
entier	entière	entièrement	*entirely*
faux	fausse	faussement	*falsely*
franc	franche	franchement	*frankly*
sérieux	sérieuse	sérieusement	*seriously*

EXERCISE B **Gilles, un enfant.** Gilles is crying. Describe what his family members are doing to calm him down. Replace the given adjectives with the corresponding adverbs.

1. (doux) Gilles pleure ——————————— .

2. (tranquille) Sa mère le berce ——————————— .

3. (attentif) Son père le touche ——————————— .

4. (timide) Sa sœur lui parle ——————————— .

5. (continuel) Gilles crie ——————————— .

6. (sérieux) Toute la famille le regarde ——————————— .

7. (correct) Enfin sa grand-mère le nourrit ——————————— .

8. (rapide) Gilles mange ——————————— .

c. Some adverbs have forms distinct from the adjective forms.

ADJECTIVE		ADVERB	
bon	*good*	**bien**	*well*
mauvais	*bad*	**mal**	*badly*
petit	*little*	**peu**	*little*

EXERCISE C **Dans une colonie de vacances.** Express what happens at camp. Use the correct form of the words in parentheses.

1. (petit, peu) La ——————————— fille joue ——————————— .

2. (mauvais, mal) L'animateur parle ——————————— du ——————————— garçon.

3. (bon, bien) Tout le monde mange ——————————— de la

——————————— nourriture.

4. (petit, peu)   Les campeurs défendent —————————— le

——————————— garçon.

5. (mauvais, mal)   Le —————————— match finit ——————————— .

6. (bon, bien)   Les —————————— directeurs dirigent ———————————

le camp.

d. Other common adverbs and adverbial expressions

alors *then*		**même** *even*	
après *afterward*		**moins** *less*	
assez *enough, quite*		**partout** *everywhere*	
aujourd'hui *today*		**peut-être** *perhaps, maybe*	
aussi *also, too*		**plus** *more*	
beaucoup *much*		**près** *near*	
bientôt *soon*		**quelquefois** *sometimes*	
déjà *already*		**souvent** *often*	
demain *tomorrow*		**surtout** *especially*	
encore *still, yet, again*		**tard** *late*	
enfin *at last*		**tôt** *soon, early*	
ensemble *together*		**toujours** *always, still*	
ensuite *then*		**tout** *quite, entirely*	
hier *yesterday*		**tout à coup** *suddenly*	
ici *here*		**tout à fait** *entirely*	
jamais *never*		**tout de suite** *immediately*	
là *there*		**très** *very*	
loin *far*		**trop** *too much*	
longtemps *a long time*		**vite** *quickly*	
maintenant *now*			

EXERCISE D   **Les contraires.**   Read the following sentences about Janine. Rewrite each sentence replacing the adverb in boldface with its opposite.

1. Janine habite **ici**.   ———————————————

2. C'est tout **près**.   ———————————————

3. Elle vient **rarement** chez moi.   ———————————————

4. Elle prend un bus qui roule très **lentement**.   ———————————————

5. Elle arrive chez moi assez **tôt**.   ———————————————

6. Elle parle **mal** le français.   ———————————————

7. Elle parle français **moins** que moi. _____

8. Elle étudie **peu** avec moi. _____

2.   Adverbs of Quantity

Certain adverbs expressing quantity are followed by *de,* without an article, when they precede a noun.

assez de   *enough*

beaucoup de   *much, many*

combien de   *how much, how many*

moins de   *less, fewer*

peu de   *little, few*

plus de   *more*

trop de   *too much, too many*

Ce prof donne *trop de* devoirs.   *That teacher gives too much homework.*

Il gagne *beaucoup d'*argent.   *He earns a lot of money.*

EXERCISE E   **Au lit.** Stéphane is home in bed, sick. Explain what he has to do.

EXAMPLE: trop/journaux à lire   Il a **trop de** journaux à lire.

1. beaucoup/livres à finir   _____

2. plus/magazines à lire   _____

3. moins/films à regarder   _____

4. peu/lettres à écrire   _____

5. assez/CD à écouter   _____

3.   Position of Adverbs

a. When modifying a verb in a simple tense, an adverb is usually placed directly after the verb it modifies.

Il *écoute attentivement.*   *He listens attentively.*

EXERCISE F   **Un entraînement.** Express what happens when Élise goes to the gym to train by putting the adverb in its correct place.

1. (attentivement) Elle écoute son entraîneur.

_____

2. (sérieusement) Elle fait ses exercices.

_____

3. (souvent)   Elle est fatiguée.

_____

4. (activement)   Elle participe.

_____

5. (énormément)   Elle maigrit.

_____

6. (drôlement)   Elle devient forte.

_____

7. (rarement)   Elle annule ses séances.

_____

8. (toujours)   Après son entraînement elle a mal au dos.

_____

b. When modifying a verb in the *passé composé* (see Chapters 17 and 18), the adverb generally follows the past participle. However, a few common adverbs, such as *bien, mal, souvent, toujours, déjà,* and *encore,* as well as adverbs of quantity, usually precede the past participle.

J'ai *cherché partout.*   *I looked everywhere.*
Nous avons *déjà mangé.*   *We have already eaten.*

EXERCISE G   **L'interview.**   Express what Georges did during his job interview by putting the adverb in its correct place.

1. (franchement)   Il a parlé.   _____
2. (souvent)   Il a regardé le directeur.   _____
3. (toujours)   Il a gardé son sang-froid.   _____
4. (sérieusement)   Il a répondu.   _____
5. (bien)   Il a expliqué son résumé.   _____
6. (attentivement) Il a écouté.   _____

EXERCISE H   **Les activités.**   Work with a partner. Take turns describing how you do five different activities.

EXAMPLE: Je joue **bien** au tennis.

_____

_____

_____

_____

_____

| EXERCISE 1 | **En classe.** Write a note to a friend describing how you act in your French class.

_____

_____

_____

_____

_____

CHAPTER 16
Reflexive Verbs

1. Reflexive Verbs in the Present Tense

a. In a reflexive construction, the action is performed by the subject upon itself. The reflexive verb has a reflexive pronoun as its direct or indirect object. Thus, the subject and the pronoun object refer to the same person(s) or thing(s). A reflexive verb can be identified by the *se* that precedes it in the infinitive. The reflexive pronoun (*me, te, se, nous, vous*) generally precedes the verb.

PRESENT TENSE			
je	*me*	**prépare**	*I prepare (am preparing) myself*
tu	*te*	**prépares**	*you prepare (are preparing) yourself*
il / elle	*se*	**prépare**	*he/she prepares (is preparing) himself/herself*
nous	*nous*	**préparons**	*we prepare (are preparing) ourselves*
vous	*vous*	**préparez**	*you prepare (are preparing) yourself/yourselves*
ils / elles	*se*	**préparent**	*they prepare (are preparing) themselves*

b. Negative, interrogative, and negative interrogative constructions follow the same rules as regular verbs. The reflexive pronouns remain before the verb.

Ils *se lèvent.*	*They get up.*
Elle ne *se lève* **pas.**	*She doesn't get up.*
*Se lève-*t-il?	*Is he getting up?*
Tu (ne) *te lèves* **(pas)?**	*Are(n't) you getting up?*
Est-ce que tu (ne) t*e lèves* **(pas)?**	

c. Common Reflexive Verbs

s'amuser   *to have a good time, fun; to enjoy oneself*

s'appeler   *to be called*

se brosser   *to brush oneself*

se coucher   *to go to bed*

se dépêcher   *to hurry*

se déshabiller   *to get undressed*

s'ennuyer   *to get bored*

s'habiller   *to get dressed*

se laver   *to wash (oneself), get washed*

se lever   *to get up; to rise*

se maquiller   *to put on make-up*

se mettre en route   *to start out*

se peigner   *to comb one's hair*

se préparer   *to prepare onself*

se promener   *to take a walk*
se rappeler   *to remember*
se raser   *to shave oneself*
se réveiller   *to wake up*

NOTE: 1.   *Me, te,* and *se* become *m', t',* and *s'* before a verb beginning with a vowel or a silent h: *il s'amuse* (he has fun); *elle s'habille* (she gets dressed).

2.   Remember the spelling changes in the *je, tu* and third person forms in certain -*er* verbs: *s'appeler: il s'appelle* (his name is); *s'ennuyer: je m'ennuie* (I get bored); *se lever: ils se lèvent* (they get up); and *se promener: elles se promènent* (they take a walk). See Chapter 7.

3.   A verb that is reflexive in French is not necessarily reflexive in English.

Je *m'habille.*   *I am getting dressed.*
Nous *nous levons.*   *We get up.*

4.   Some reflexive verbs may be used with a direct object in addition to the reflexive pronoun (which serves as an indirect object). This direct object often denotes a part of the body.

Il se lave la figure.   *He washes his face.*

5.   Most transitive verbs can become reflexive verbs when used with the reflexive pronoun.

se parler   *to speak to oneself*   **se regarder**   *to look at oneself*

EXERCISE A   **On sort.**   Express what the following people do before going out.

EXAMPLE: elle/se réveiller de sa sieste   Elle se réveille de sa sieste.

1. vous/se peigner   _____

2. nous/s'habiller   _____

3. ils/se brosser les dents   _____

4. je/se maquiller   _____

5. elle/se laver   _____

6. tu/se préparer   _____

7. il/se raser   _____

8. elles/se dépêcher   _____

EXERCISE B   **La routine.**   Complete the sentences showing what each person does by using an appropriate reflexive pronoun where necessary.

1. Tu ——— promènes et tu ——— promènes ton chien.

2. Ils ——— rasent leur chien et ils ——— rasent.

3. Nous ——— lavons la voiture et nous ——— lavons.

4. Vous ——— habillez et vous ——— habillez votre enfant.

5. Je ——— lève la main et je ——— lève.

6. Elles ——— peignent et elles ——— peignent leurs poupées.

7. Il ——— appelle Bruno et il ——— appelle son ami.

8. Elle ——— couche le bébé et elle ——— couche.

EXERCISE C   **Tout seul.**   Ask what different people do when they are alone and then give their negative answers.

EXAMPLE: il/se préparer un hamburger.
         Il **se prépare** un hamburger? Il **ne se prépare pas** de hamburger.

1. tu/se parler   _____

2. elle/se regarder dans le miroir   _____

3. nous/se comparer aux autres   _____

4. ils/se coucher tôt   _____

5. vous/s'ennuyer   _____

6. je/s'organiser   _____

2.   Reflexive Constructions With Infinitives

When the reflexive verb is in the infinitive, the reflexive pronoun precedes the infinitive and agrees with the subject of the sentence.

Je vais m'acheter un cadeau.   *I'm going to buy myself a present.*
Elle ne veut pas se lever tôt.   *She doesn't want to get up early.*

EXERCISE D   **Quand?**   Express at what time each person likes to do the listed activities on a school day.

EXAMPLE: il/se peigner   Il aime **se peigner à huit heures.**

1. tu/se brosser les dents   _____

2. vous/se laver   _____

3. je/s'habiller   _____

4. ils/se coucher _____

5. elle/se réveiller _____

6. nous/mettre en route _____

EXERCISE E **Les vacances.** It's time to take a break from work. Express what these people don't feel like doing.

> se réveiller à six heures
> se coucher très tôt
> se mettre en route à sept heures et demie
> se laver la figure à sept heures
> s'habiller à six heures et demie
> se préparer à quitter la maison si tôt

EXAMPLE: Il n'a pas envie de se brosser les dents à sept heures.

1. Je _____.

2. Tu _____.

3. Nous _____.

4. Elle _____.

5. Vous _____.

6. Ils _____.

3. Reflexive Commands

In affirmative commands, reflexive pronouns follow the verb and *toi* is used instead of *te.* In negative commands, reflexive pronouns precede the imperative.

AFFIRMATIVE COMMAND	
Couche-toi!	*Go to bed!*
Couchez-vous!	*Go to bed!*
Couchons-nous!	*Let's go to bed!*

NEGATIVE COMMAND	
Ne te couche pas!	*Don't go to bed!*
Ne vous couchez pas!	*Don't go to bed!*
Ne nous couchons pas!	*Let's not go to bed!*

EXERCISE F **Les conseils.** Write the affirmative and negative advice a friend gives you.

EXAMPLE: s'habiller/se maquiller **Habille-toi! Ne te maquille pas!**

1. se coucher/ se lever

_____

2. se peigner/se brosser les cheveux

_____

3. s'amuser/s'ennuyer

_____

4. se préparer/se dépêcher

_____

EXERCISE G   **Attention, les enfants!**   Your mother is going out and you are babysitting for your younger brothers and sisters. Write what your mother tells them.

EXAMPLE: se laver à six heures/à neuf heures
Ne vous lavez pas à six heures. **Lavez-vous à** neuf heures.

1. se coucher/trop tard/tôt

_____

2. se brosser les dents avant le dîner/après le dîner

_____

3. se déshabiller à cinq heures/à huit heures et demie

_____

4. se promener après le dîner/avant le dîner

_____

EXERCISE H   **Au parc d'attractions.**   Read the ad then tell why you might want to visit this place.

PARC D'ATTRACTIONS FANTAISIE
AMUSEZ-VOUS CHEZ NOUS!

Dépêchez-vous de nous rendre visite!
Laissez-vous tenter par une multitude d'activités liées
aux sports, aux loisirs et à l'imagination.
Un parc exceptionnel pour les enfants de tous les âges à découvrir.

_____

_____

_____

_____

_____

| EXERCISE I | **Chacun son tour!** Work with a partner. Take turns giving each other commands and acting them out.

_____

_____

_____

_____

_____

| EXERCISE J | **Le retard.** You have made a resolution to turn over a new leaf and to be always on time. Write a note to your parents telling them what you plan on doing to fulfill your obligation.

_____

_____

_____

_____

_____

CHAPTER 17
Passé composé of *avoir* Verbs

1. Affirmative Construction of Regular Verbs

The *passé composé* is a past tense composed of two parts: the present tense of the auxiliary verb, or "helping" verb, and the past participle of the main verb. For most verbs, the auxiliary verb is *avoir* (to have).

parler *to speak*			choisir *to choose*			attendre *to wait*		
I spoke, I have spoken			*I chose, I have chosen*			*I waited, I have waited*		
j'	ai	parlé	j'	ai	choisi	j'	ai	attendu
tu	as	parlé	tu	as	choisi	tu	as	attendu
il/elle	a	parlé	il/elle	a	choisi	il/elle	a	attendu
nous	avons	parlé	nous	avons	choisi	nous	avons	attendu
vous	avez	parlé	vous	avez	choisi	vous	avez	attendu
ils/elles	ont	parlé	ils/elles	ont	choisi	ils/elles	ont	attendu

NOTE: 1. The past participle of *–er* verbs is formed by dropping *–er* and adding *é*.

J'ai jou*é* avec l'ordinateur.	*I played on the computer.*
Elle a achet*é* des CD.	*She bought CDs.*

2. The past participle of *–ir* verbs is formed by dropping the *–r*.

Il a fin*i* son travail.	*He finished his work.*
Elle a maigr*i*.	*She lost weight.*

3. The past participle of *–re* verbs is formed by dropping *–re* and adding *–u*.

Ils ont vend*u* leur voiture.	*They sold their car.*
J'ai perd*u* mon stylo.	*I lost my pen.*

EXERCISE A   **Le pique-nique.**   Express what each family member did at the picnic.

EXAMPLE: papa/trouver un bon endroit pour le pique-nique
Papa **a trouvé** un bon endroit pour le pique-nique.

1. je/allumer le feu

_____

2. maman/cuisiner les hamburgers

_____

3. mes frères/jouer au base-ball

_____

4. ma sœur et moi/préparer la salade

_____

5. vous/apporter les sandwiches

_____

6. tu/distribuer les glaces

_____

EXERCISE B   **Au gymnase.** Express what each person at the gym did.

EXAMPLE: Maryse/choisir un entraîneur
           Maryse **a choisi** un entraîneur.

1. tu / maigrir

_____

2. Mathieu / grossir un peu

_____

3. elles / finir leurs exercices

_____

4. je / applaudir son succès

_____

5. vous / obéir à votre entraîneur

_____

6. nous / désobéir à nos amis

_____

EXERCISE C   **Les commérages.** Express what happened when gossip began to spread.

EXAMPLE: (attendre) Lucette _____ une réponse de Catherine.
           Lucette **a attendu** une réponse de Catherine.

1. (entendre)   Vous _____ des histoires horribles.

2. (défendre)   Elles _____ leurs amies.

3. (correspondre) Tu _____ avec d'autres personnes.

4. (répondre)   Je _____ gentiment.

5. (perdre)   Nous _____ du respect pour Jacqueline.

6. (rendre)   Il _____ visite à Catherine.

2. Affirmative Construction of Irregular Verbs

All irregular verbs follow the same rules as regular verbs in the passé composé. The following verbs have irregular past participles:

INFINITIVE		PAST PARTICIPLE	INFINITIVE		PAST PARTICIPLE
apprendre	to learn	appris	mettre	to put	mis
avoir	to have	eu	ouvrir	to open	ouvert
comprendre	to understand	compris	pouvoir	to be able	pu
dire	to say	dit	prendre	to take	pris
écrire	to write	écrit	recevoir	to receive	reçu
être	to be	été	savoir	to know	su
faire	to make, do	fait	voir	to see	vu
lire	to read	lu	vouloir	to want	voulu

J'*ai lu* un très bon livre.   *I read a very good book.*

Ils *ont fait* un voyage.   *They took a trip.*

EXERCISE D   **Pour la première fois.**   Express what each person did for the first time.

EXAMPLE: Boris/dire la vérité   Boris **a dit** la vérité.

1. Roxane et Rosalie/voir leur grands-parents

   _____

2. je/recevoir la meilleure note

   _____

3. nous/comprendre la leçon de maths

   _____

4. tu/être à l'heure

   _____

5. le bébé/pouvoir marcher tout seul

   _____

6. Fabien/mettre de l'argent de côté

   _____

7. Thomas et Fernand/faire un voyage en bateau

   _____

8. Charline/écrire une lettre à son correspondant

   _____

3.   Uses of the *passé composé*

The *passé composé* is used to narrate an action or event completed in the past. Note the English equivalents of the *passé composé*:

J'*ai reçu une lettre importante.**	*I (have) received an important letter.*
Nous *avons fait* du tennis.	*We played tennis.*

NOTE: 1.   When modifying a verb in the *passé composé*, the adverb generally follows the past participle. However, a few common adverbs, such as *bien, mal, souvent, toujours, déjà*, and *encore*, as well as adverbs of quantity, usually precede the past participle.

Il a *travaillé vite*.	*He worked quickly.*
Je n'ai pas *encore vu* ce film.	*I haven't seen that film yet.*
J'ai *beaucoup mangé*.	*I ate a lot.*

2.   Some expressions that are often used with the *passé composé* are:

l'année passée, l'année dernière   *last year*

avant-hier   *the day before yesterday*

hier   *yesterday*

hier soir   *last night*

le mois passé, le mois dernier   *last month*

la semaine passée, la semaine dernière   *last week*

EXERCISE E   **Dimanche dernier.**   Complete the story by providing the correct form of the *passé composé* of the verb indicated.

Dimanche dernier mon mari et moi _____ 1. (rendre) visite à mon fils, Michel, qui

_____ 2. (réussir) à devenir officier à bord d'un sous-marin. Son équipage et lui _____ 3. (faire)

escale dans l'État de Connecticut. Nous _____ 4. (décider) d'y aller parce que, ce jour-là,

Michel _____ 5. (vouloir) nous montrer son bateau. Il _____ 6. (attendre) notre arrivée avec

impatience. Nous _____ 7. (prendre) la voiture, et à cause de la circulation le voyage au

Connecticut _____ 8. (durer) plus de deux heures. À la base sous-marine, un garde

_____ 9. (vérifier) notre voiture et nos papiers. Finalement tout le monde _____ 10. (recevoir)

mon mari et moi à bord du bateau et Michel _____ 11. (présenter) son père et moi à tous ses

collègues. Puis il _____ 12. (montrer) comment le sous-marin fonctionne. Nous _____ 13. (apprendre)

pas mal de choses ce dimanche matin. À une heure et demie, nous _____ 14. (avoir) faim et

nous _____ 15. (quitter) le bateau pour aller manger. Heureusement nous _____ 16. (déjeuner)

dans un restaurant qui ————————— le plat préféré de Michel. Ce jour-là tout le monde
                              17. (servir)

————————————— très content.
  18. (être)

4. Negative and Interrogative Constructions

a. In a negative sentence in the *passé composé*, *ne* precedes the helping verb and the negative word follows it.

Je *n'ai pas* compris les devoirs.   *I didn't understand the homework.*

Il *n'a jamais* joué au football.   *He never played soccer.*

b. A question may be indicated with intonation alone, or it can be formed by beginning the sentence with *est-ce que*.

Tu as lavé la voiture?   *Did you wash the car?*

***Est-ce qu'*elle a réussi?**   *Did she succeed?*

Inversion may also be used in the *passé composé* by inverting the subject pronoun and the auxiliary verb.

***Avez-vous* pris le métro?**   *Did you take the subway?*

***A-t-il* rangé le salon?**   *Did he straighten the living room?*

EXERCISE F   **Les préparatifs.** Express what these people have and haven't done to prepare for a concert they are giving.

EXAMPLES: Luc/écouter la musique (oui)

Luc **a écouté** la musique.

Marie/acheter un nouveau violon (non)

Marie **n'a pas acheté** un nouveau violon.

1. vous/choisir votre musique (non)

   _____

2. tu/jouer le morceau de musique (oui)

   _____

3. je/répéter le second mouvement (non)

   _____

4. nous/acheter de nouveaux vêtements (oui)

   _____

5. Guillaume/envoyer des invitations à sa famille (oui)

   _____

6. Laure et Benjamin/corriger leurs fautes (non)

   _____

7. Diane et Christine/perdre confiance (non)

_____

8. on/commencer à s'inquiéter (oui)

_____

| EXERCISE G | **Jamais de la vie.** You and a friend are discussing things you've never done in your life. Express the questions and the answers. |

EXAMPLE: apprendre une langue étrangère

    AMI: **As-tu jamais appris** une langue étrangère?

    VOUS: **Non, je n'ai jamais appris** de langue étrangère.

1. écrire un poème

    AMI: _____

    VOUS: _____

2. lire un roman français

    AMI: _____

    VOUS: _____

3. voir une pièce

    AMI: _____

    VOUS: _____

4. recevoir un A en maths

    AMI: _____

    VOUS: _____

5. vouloir voyager

    AMI: _____

    VOUS: _____

6. avoir un correspondant

    AMI: _____

    VOUS: _____

7. pouvoir nager

    AMI: _____

    VOUS: _____

8. savoir taper à la machine

   AMI: _____

   VOUS: _____

9. ouvrir un compte en banque

   AMI: _____

   VOUS: _____

10. prendre l'avion

   AMI: _____

   VOUS: _____

   c. A negative interrogative sentence in the *passé composé* may be indicated with intonation alone, or it can be formed by beginning the sentence with *est-ce que.*

   Philippe n'a pas gagné le match?   *Didn't Philippe win the match?*
   Est-ce que **Philippe n'a pas gagné le match?**   *Didn't Philippe win the match?*

EXERCISE H   **Un voyage en France.**   Your French class took a trip to France. Write the questions your parents ask you when you return home and your answers.

EXAMPLES: passer de bonnes vacances (oui)
   Est-ce que tu n'as pas passé de bonnes vacances?
   Mais si, **j'ai passé** de bonnes vacances.

   parler français tout le temps (non)
   Est-ce que tu **n'as pas parlé** français tout le temps?
   Non, je **n'ai pas parlé** français tout le temps.

1. manger les cuisses de grenouille (non)

   _____

   _____

2. acheter des souvenirs (oui)

   _____

   _____

3. regarder des films français (non)

   _____

   _____

4. voir la Tour Eiffel (oui)

   _____

   _____

5. visiter le Louvre (oui)

   _____

   _____

6. faire une promenade aux Champs Élysées (non)

   _____

   _____

7. être aux Invalides (oui)

   _____

   _____

8. célébrer le quatorze juillet à Montmartre (non)

   _____

   _____

9. saisir l'occasion d'aller voir la Sainte-Chapelle (oui)

   _____

   _____

10. prendre un bateau mouche (non)

    _____

    _____

| EXERCISE I | **Après l'école.** Work with a partner. Take turns saying what you did after school yesterday. List five activities. |

_____

_____

_____

| EXERCISE J | Write a note to a friend explaining why you couldn't go out with her last weekend. Explain what you did and why. |

_____

_____

_____

CHAPTER 18
Passé composé of *être* Verbs

1. Verbs Conjugated With *être*

Sixteen common verbs use the helping verb *être* instead of *avoir*. Their *passé composé* is formed by conjugating the present tense of *être* and the past participle of the verb. Most of these verbs express motion or change of place or state.

INFINITIVE	PAST PARTICIPLE	INFINITIVE	PAST PARTICIPLE
aller *to go*	**allé**	**naître** *to be born*	**né**
venir *to come*	**venu**	**mourir** *to die*	**mort**
arriver *to arrive*	**arrivé**	**rentrer** *to go in again, return*	**rentré**
partir *to leave, go away*	**parti**	**retourner** *to go back, return*	**retourné**
entrer *to enter*	**entré**	**revenir** *to come back*	**revenu**
sortir *to go out, leave*	**sorti**	**rester** *to remain, stay*	**resté**
monter *to go up, come up*	**monté**	**devenir** *to become*	**devenu**
descendre *to go down*	**descendu**	**tomber** *to fall*	**tombé**

2. Agreement of Past Participles

Past participles of verbs conjugated with *être* agree in gender (masculine or feminine) and number (singular or plural) with the subject.

MASCULINE SUBJECTS	FEMININE SUBJECTS	MEANING
je suis allé	je suis allée	*I went*
tu es allé	tu es allée	*you went*
il est allé	elle est allée	*he/she went*
nous sommes allés	nous sommes allées	*we went*
vous êtes allé(s)	vous êtes allée(s)	*you went*
ils sont allés	elles sont allées	*they went*

Marie est *née* en France.   *Marie was born in France.*

Ils sont *venus* en retard.   *They came late.*

NOTE: 1. When the subject is both masculine and feminine, the past participle is masculine plural.

   Grégoire et Lise sont *sortis*.   *Grégoire and Lise went out.*

2. Since the pronouns *je, tu, nous,* and *vous* may be masculine or feminine, and *vous* may be singular or plural, the past participles used with them vary in endings.

EXERCISE A   **On fait les courses.**   Express where each person went.

EXAMPLE: Pierre **est allé à l'épicerie.**

1. Je _____.

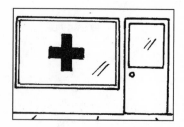

2. Nous _____.

3. Anne et toi, vous _____.

4. Les filles _____.

5. Jacques et Érica _____.

6. Patricia _____.

EXERCISE B | **La semaine passée.** Complete the story with the correct forms of the verbs indicated in the *passé composé*.

La semaine passée maman _____ à l'hôpital avec papa. Papa _____

1. (aller) .... 2. (devenir)

nerveux. Ils _____ de notre maison à sept heures. Ils _____ dans

3. (partir) .... 4. (entrer)

la salle d'attente mais peu de temps après, ils _____ au troisième étage. À neuf

5. (monter)

heures ma sœur Hélène _____ . Maman et Hélène _____ à l'hôpital

6. (naître) .... 7. (rester)

pendant deux jours. L'après-midi du deuxième jour, mes parents et Hélène _____

8. (descendre)

et ils _____ chez nous tout de suite.

9. (rentrer)

3. Negative, interrogative, and negative interrogative forms of the *passé composé* of verbs conjugated with *être* are:

Elle *n'est pas rentrée*.	*She didn't return.*

Elle *est rentrée?*	
Est-ce qu'*elle *est rentrée?	*Did she return?*
Est-*elle *rentrée?	

Elle *n'est pas rentrée?*	
Est-ce qu'*elle *n'est pas rentrée?	*Didn't she return?*

EXERCISE C | **On désobéit.** Express why these people's parents became angry with them.

EXAMPLE: Georges/rester à la maison

Georges **n'est pas resté** à la maison.

1. Grégoire/rentrer à l'heure

_____

2. Claire/devenir sérieuse

_____

3. Jean-Luc et Gérard/arriver à la maison pour dîner en famille

_____

4. Adèle et Caroline/aller en ville faire les courses

_____

5. Gisèle et Albert/monter dans leurs chambres faire leurs devoirs

_____

6. Michelle/descendre pour faire le ménage

_____

7. Micheline et Jeanne/partir à l'école à l'heure

_____

8. Michel et Éric/revenir du concert avant minuit

_____

| EXERCISE D | **Le témoignage.** You witnessed an accident. Write the questions that you are asked by the authorities and give an affirmative or negative answer as indicated. |

EXAMPLE: (le premier conducteur) sortir facilement de sa voiture (oui)
Est-il sorti facilement de sa voiture?
Oui, il **est sorti** facilement de sa voiture.

(le deuxième conducteur) rester dans sa voiture (non)
Est-il resté dans sa voiture?
Non, il **n'est pas resté** dans sa voiture.

1. (une passagère) mourir (non)

_____

_____

2. (les ambulances) arriver sur place tout de suite (oui)

_____

_____

3. (les autres passagers) sortir immédiatement de la voiture (oui)

_____

_____

4. (le premier conducteur) aller téléphoner à la police (non)

_____

_____

5. (le deuxiéme conducteur) entrer dans un café pour téléphoner à sa femme (non)

_____

_____

6. (la police) venir (oui)

_____

_____

7. (deux passagères) retourner dans leur voiture (non)

_____

_____

8. (une ambulance) partir (oui)

_____

_____

EXERCISE E Complete the story using the correct helping verb and past participle for the verbs indicated.

Hier je (j') _____ 1. (décider) d'acheter une nouvelle voiture. Alors je (j') _____ 2. (téléphoner)

à un ami et je (j') _____ 3. (partir) le chercher tout de suite. Nous _____ 4. (descendre) en

ville où il y a pas mal de magasins de voitures. Nous _____ 5. (aller) à un grand magasin

et nous y _____ 6. (entrer) . Un vendeur _____ 7. (arriver) immédiatement nous mon-

trer sa nouvelle ligne de voitures. Je (J') _____ 8. (voir) la voiture de mes rêves – une jolie

voiture de sport rouge. Le vendeur _____ 9. (ouvrir) la portière de cette beauté et mon ami

et moi _____ 10. (regarder) à l'intérieur. Quelle voiture formidable! Je (J') _____ 11. (demander)

le prix au vendeur. Au début il ne (n') _____ 12. (vouloir) révéler le prix. Il _____ 13. (suggérer)

que cette voiture coûte très cher. Enfin il _____ 14. (dit) soixante-quinze mille dollars!

Je (J') _____ 15. (être) complètement étourdi. Je ne (n') _____ 16. (attendre) un tel prix.

Alors, je (j') _____ 17. (prendre) la décision de ne pas acheter de voiture ce jour-là, et mon ami

et moi _____ 18. (sortir) du magasin.

| EXERCISE F | **Le week-end.** Work with a partner. Take turns asking each other where you went and what you did over the week-end. Consider six situations. |

_____

_____

_____

_____

_____

_____

| EXERCISE G | **Les vacances.** Write a letter to a friend telling where you went and what you did on your last vacation. |

_____

_____

_____

_____

_____

_____

CHAPTER 19
Imperfect Tense

1. Regular Verbs

The imperfect tense (*l'imparfait*) of regular verbs is formed by dropping the *–ons* ending of the *nous* form of the present tense and adding the imperfect tense endings *-ais, -ais, -ait, -ions, -iez, -aient*.

parler *to speak*	**finir** *to finish*	**vendre** *to sell*
nous parlons	**nous finissons**	**nous vendons**
I spoke, I was speaking, I used to speak, etc.	I finished, I was finishing, I used to finish, etc.	I sold, I was selling, I used to sell, etc.
je parl*ais* tu parl*ais* il / elle parl*ait* nous parl*ions* vous parl*iez* ils / elles parl*aient*	je finiss*ais* tu finiss*ais* il / elle finiss*ait* nous finiss*ions* vous finiss*iez* ils / elles finiss*aient*	je vend*ais* tu vend*ais* il / elle vend*ait* nous vend*ions* vous vend*iez* ils / elles vend*aient*

NOTE: 1. Verbs ending in *–ions* and *–iez* in the present tense end in *–iions* and *–iiez* in the imperfect tense: *nous étudiions, vous étudiiez.*

2. Negative, interrogative, and negative interrogative constructions in the imperfect follow the same rules as in the present tense.

Bernard ne travaillait pas.	*Bernard wasn't working.*
Tu rougissais?	*Were you blushing?*
Est-ce qu'elle attendait?	*Was she waiting?*
Dansaient-ils?	*Were they dancing?*
Vous n'aimiez pas aller à la plage?	*Didn't you like to go to the beach?*
Est-ce que tu ne jouais pas du piano?	*Didn't you used to play the piano?*

| **EXERCISE A** | **La mode d'autrefois.** Express what these different people used to wear in the past. |

EXAMPLE: il/préférer/les bermudas
     Il **préférait** les bermudas.

1. nous/aimer/les pantalons à pattes

---

2. tu/porter/des chaussures à plate-forme

_____

3. je/chercher/des pantalons troués

_____

4. vous/demander/une maxi-jupe

_____

5. ils/désirer/un col Nehru

_____

6. elle/parler/des micro-mini-jupes

_____

EXERCISE B **Des enfants terribles.** Ask questions about what those children used to do by using the imperfect.

EXAMPLES: (Douglas) bâtir des édifices de carton dans le salon
Bâtissait-il des édifices de carton dans le salon?

(Anne) ne pas travailler dans un café
Ne travaillait-elle pas dans un café?

1. (Raymond et Lise) désobéir à leurs parents.

_____

2. (Bernadette) ne jamais finir ses repas

_____

3. (Claude) remplir la piscine de sable

_____

4. (Bertrand et Alexandre) ne jamais choisir la réponse correcte

_____

5. (Annette et Nathalie) ne pas réussir à faire de leur mieux

_____

6. (Josiane) punir son petit frère continuellement

_____

EXERCISE C **Jamais plus.** Express what these people were no longer waiting for.

EXAMPLE: Georgette/des surprises
Georgette **n'attendait plus de** surprises.

1. je/un coup de téléphone

_____

2. Lucien/ une surprise-partie

_____

3. nous/ des lettres de nos correspondants

_____

4. vous/une carte d'anniversaire

_____

5. Renée et Valérie/une augmentation de salaire

_____

6. tu/les prochaines vacances

_____

| EXERCISE D | **Une panne d'électricité.**   There was a blackout. Express what these people were doing when the lights went out. |

1. (finir)   Nous _____ notre déjeuner.

2. (attendre)   Je (J') _____ le bus.

3. (étudier)   Madeleine _____ .

4. (jouer)   Louis et Stéphane _____ au basket.

5. (remplir)   Vous _____ un formulaire.

6. (descendre) Tu _____ en ville.

2.   Spelling Changes in Certain –er Verbs

a. Verbs ending in _–cer_ change _c_ to _ç_ before _a_ to keep the soft _c_ sound.

placer _to place_	
je plaçais	nous placions
tu plaçais	vous placiez
il/elle plaçait	ils/elles plaçaient

b. Verbs ending in _–ger_ insert silent _e_ between _g_ and _a_ to keep the soft _g_ sound.

nager _to swim_	
je nageais	nous nagions
tu nageais	vous nagiez
il/elle nageait	ils/elles nageaient

EXERCISE E | **Les babysitters.** You and your friends are babysitting for a neighbor's children, who were misbehaving. Express what was going on.

EXAMPLE: Jules/avancer continuellement le film dans le magnétoscope
Jules **avançait** continuellement le film dans le magnétoscope.

1. je/menacer de téléphoner à leurs parents

_____

2. tu/effacer les dessins au crayon sur les murs

_____

3. Salomé/renoncer à se comporter bien

_____

4. nous/prononcer les règles fréquemment

_____

5. ils/lancer des macaronis

_____

6. vous/annoncer le retour de leurs parents

_____

EXERCISE F | **Le goûter.** Express what these people were eating for a snack.

EXAMPLE: Il **mangeait des bonbons.**

1. Tu _____ . 2. Vous _____ .

3. Je _____ .

4. Ils _____ .

5. Nous_____ .

6. Elle _____ .

3. Imperfect of Irregular Verbs

The imperfect of irregular verbs, with few exceptions, is formed in the same way as the imperfect of regular verbs.

INFINITIVE	PRESENT *NOUS* FORM	IMPERFECT
avoir *to have*	**avons**	j'avais, tu avais, il / elle avait nous avions, vous aviez, ils / elles avaient
aller *to go*	**allons**	j'allais, tu allais, il / elle allait nous allions, vous alliez, ils / elles allaient
faire *to do*	**faisons**	je faisais, tu faisais, il / elle faisait nous faisions, vous faisiez, ils / elles faisaient
venir *to come*	**venons**	je venais, tu venais, il / elle venait nous venions, vous veniez, ils / elles venaient
voir *to see*	**voyons**	je voyais, tu voyais, il / elle voyait nous voyions, vous voyiez, ils / elles voyaient

NOTE: In the imperfect, *être* (to be) adds regular endings to an irregular stem.

j'étais	nous étions
tu étais	vous étiez
il/elle était	ils/elles étaient

EXERCISE G | Les sentiments. Express how these people felt.

consciencieux   égoïste   intuitif   poli
courageux   franc   malheureux

EXAMPLE: Janine sauvait la vie à Raoul.   Elle **était courageuse.**

1. Georgette et Marie pleuraient.   _____

2. Je travaillais dur.   _____

3. Lucien ne partageait rien avec ses amis.   _____

4. Vous saviez ce que tout le monde pensait.   _____

5. Nous disions toujours merci.   _____

6. Tu écrivais toujours la vérité.   _____

EXERCISE H | Des enfants gâtés.   Complete the sentences about spoiled children by filling in the correct form of the proper verb in the imperfect.

EXAMPLE: (demander/désirer) Elle **demandait** tout ce qu'elle **désirait.**

1. (recevoir/vouloir) Il _____ tout ce qu'il _____ .

2. (voir/jouer) Nous _____ tous les films qu'on _____ .

3. (faire/pouvoir) Mme Dutour _____ tous les voyages

   qu'elle _____ .

4. (aller/avoir) Je _____ à tous les concerts qu'il y _____ .

5. (manger/acheter) Elle _____ tous les chocolats que sa mère

   _____ .

6. (essayer/vendre) Elles _____ toutes les robes que cette boutique

   _____ .

7. (venir/donner) Vous _____ à toutes les fêtes qu'on _____ .

8. (prendre/offrir) Ils _____ tout l'argent que leur père leur

   _____ .

4.   Uses of the Imperfect

The imperfect tense expresses actions, circumstances, events, and situations that were continuous, repeated, or habitual in the past.

a. The imperfect describes what was happening, used to happen, or happened repeatedly in the past.

Les élèves *rigolaient*.	*The students were joking around.*
Il *habitait* en France.	*He lived (used to live) in France.*
Je *travaillais* chaque jour.	*I worked (would work, used to work) every day.*

> **NOTE:** The imperfect tense is usually equivalent to the English *was/were* + *-ing* form of the verb and to the English *used to*, and *would* (meaning *used to*).

b. The imperfect describes persons, things, or conditions in the past.

Elle était charmante.	*She was charming.*
La porte était fermée.	*The door was closed.*
Il faisait chaud.	*It was cold.*

c. The imperfect is used to express the day, the month, and the time of day in the past.

C'était dimanche.	*It was Sunday.*
C'était le mois de juillet.	*It was July.*
Il était midi.	*It was noon.*

d. The imperfect describes a situation or circumstance that was going on in the past when some single action or event occurred; this action or event is expressed in the *passé composé*.

Je *sortais* quand il m'a téléphoné.	*I was leaving when he called me.*
Il *pleuvait* quand nous sommes sortis du cinéma.	*It was raining when we left the movies.*

> **NOTE:** Two actions going on simultaneously in the past are both expressed in the imperfect.
>
> | | |
> |---|---|
> | Il *dormait* pendant que je *travaillais*. | *He was sleeping while I was working.* |
> | Pendant que je *conduisais*, j'*écoutais* la radio. | *While I was driving I was listening to the radio.* |

EXERCISE I   **Temps variable.**   Tell what these people did while on vacation under various weather conditions.

EXAMPLE: faire mauvais/je/regarder la télévision

Quand il faisait mauvais **je regardais** la télévision.

1. faire du vent/nous/faire de la voile

_____

2. faire frais/vous/monter à cheval

_____

3. faire très chaud/je/nager

_____

4. pleuvoir/elles/lire dans leur chambre

_____

5. faire du soleil/tu/aller à la plage

_____

6. faire beau/il/prendre un bain de soleil

_____

<hr>

EXERCISE J   Express what each person used to do on Saturdays.

EXAMPLE: Pierre / nager le matin
             Pierre **nageait** le matin.

1. Paul / faire ses devoirs

_____

2. ma sœur et moi / rendre visite à notre grand-mère

_____

3. tu / aller faire des achats au centre commercial

_____

4. je / manger dans un restaurant avec ma famille

_____

5. Charlotte et lui / voir des amis

_____

6. vous / écrire des lettres

_____

<hr>

EXERCISE K   **Une interruption.** Express how each person was interrupted while doing
something. Use the imperfect and the _passé composé._

EXAMPLE: il/écouter des CDs/il/entendre ses amis dehors
             Il **écoutait** des CDs quand il **a entendu** ses amis dehors.

1. je/vouloir me coucher/mon téléphone/sonner

_____

2. nous/faire un pique-nique/un orage/éclater

_____

3. tu/manger/des amis/arriver chez toi

_____

4. elle/regarder son émission favorite/son enfant/lui poser une question

_____

5. tu/te reposer/un ami/appeler

_____

6. ils/jouer avec l'ordinateur/leurs parents/rentrer

_____

EXERCISE L   **L'album de photos.**   Describe a picture in the photo album by crossing out the verbs in the present and replacing them with the imperfect.

C'est _____ 1. _____ le vingt-neuf juillet. Il **est** _____ 2. _____ trois heures de l'après-midi. Il **fait** _____ 3. _____ beau. Le ciel **est** _____ 4. _____ bleu et il n'y **a** _____ 5. _____ pas de nuages. Nous **sommes** _____ 6. _____ dans le jardin de ma sœur. Son mari et elle **préparent** _____ 7. _____ un barbecue. Mon mari les **aide** _____ 8. _____ . Ma mère **est** _____ 9. _____ assise dans une chaise longue. Elle **tricote** _____ 10. _____ un pull. Mon père **lit** _____ 11. _____ le journal. Mon neveu et mes fils **nagent** _____ 12. _____ dans la piscine. C'est _____ 13. _____ moi qui les **surveille** _____ 14. _____ et qui **prends** _____ 15. _____ la photo. Nous **célébrons** _____ 16. _____ l'anniversaire de mon père. Il **a** _____ 17. _____ quatre-vingt-sept ans. Tout le monde **s'amuse** _____ 18. _____ .

EXERCISE M   **Les réactions.**   Work with a partner. Take turns expressing how you felt when certain things happened to you. Consider six different occasions.

EXAMPLE: J'**étais nerveux** (nerveuse) quand j'**ai passé** mon examen de maths.

_____
_____
_____
_____
_____

| EXERCISE N | Une photo. Write a letter to a friend describing a photo you took. |

_____

_____

_____

_____

_____

CHAPTER 20
Future Tense

1. *Aller* + Infinitive

In French as in English, the near future may be expressed with a form of the present tense of the verb *aller* (to be going to) plus the infinitive.

Je vais manger.	*I am going to eat.*
Il va aller en ville.	*He is going to go downtown.*

The negative construction is:

Nous n'allons pas jouer au tennis.	*We aren't going to play tennis.*

The interrogative constructions are:

Tu vas sortir?	*Are you going to go out?*
Est-ce qu'ils vont jouer au basket?	*Are they going to play basketball?*
À quelle heure allez-vous partir?	*At what time are you going to leave?*

EXERCISE A | **Les métiers.** Ask what these people plan or don't plan to do. Then give answers to the questions as indicated.

EXAMPLES: elle/vendeuse/vendre des voitures (oui)
Va-t-elle devenir vendeuse? Oui, **elle va vendre** des voitures.

il/cuisinier/préparer des plats spéciaux (non)
Va-t-il devenir cuisinier? Non, **il ne va pas préparer** de plats spéciaux.

1. tu/professeur/enseigner les maths (oui)

   _____

2. ils/docteurs/guérir les malades (non)

   _____

3. vous/mécanicien/réparer les voitures (non)

   _____

4. nous/savants/faire des expériences médicales (oui)

   _____

5. elles/directrices/diriger de grandes sociétés (non)

   _____

6. il/soldat/défendre son pays (oui)

   _____

2.   Future Tense of Regular Verbs

The future tense is formed by adding the following endings to the infinitive: *-ai, -as, -a, -ons, -ez, -ont.*

jouer *to play*	**finir** *to finish*	**rendre** *to return*
I will/shall play	I will/shall finish	I will/shall return
je jouer*ai*	je finir*ai*	je rendr*ai*
tu jouer*as*	tu finir*as*	tu rendr*as*
il/elle jouer*a*	il/elle finir*a*	il/elle rendr*a*
nous jouer*ons*	nous finir*ons*	nous rendr*ons*
vous jouer*ez*	vous finir*ez*	vous rendr*ez*
ils/elles jouer*ont*	ils/elles finir*ont*	ils/elles rendr*ont*

NOTE: 1. Verbs ending in *–re* drop the final *e* before the future ending.

vendre   je vendrai   prendre   je prendrai

2. Negative, interrogative, and negative interrogative constructions in the future follow the same rules as in the present tense.

Je ne téléphonerai pas à Claude.   *I won't call Claude.*

Tu sortiras ce soir?
Est-ce que tu sortiras ce soir?   } *Will you go out tonight?*
Sortiras-tu ce soir?

Vous ne vendrez pas votre voiture?   *You won't sell your car?*

Est-ce que vous ne vendrez pas   *Won't you sell your car?*
votre voiture?

| EXERCISE B | **Les plans.**   Complete what you will do under the following circumstances by using the future tense. |

EXAMPLE: Si je fais un voyage, **je visiterai Paris.**

1. Si mon ami vient, _____ .

2. S'il pleut, _____ .

3. S'il n'y a pas de classe, _____ .

4. Si mes parents me donnent la permission, _____ .

5. Si je suis malade, _____ .

6. Si je reçois de l'argent pour mon anniversaire, _____ .

| EXERCISE C | **Les travaux domestiques.**   Express what each person will do. |

EXAMPLE: (cuisiner) **Il cuisinera.**

1. (laver)   Je _____ la voiture.

2. (arroser)   Mon frère _____ le jardin.

3. (préparer)   Mes sœurs _____ le dîner.

4. (ranger)   Mon père et moi _____ le salon.

5. (passer)   Vous _____ l'aspirateur.

6. (débarasser)   Tu _____ la table.

7. (garder)   Maman _____ les enfants.

8. (vider)   Mon oncle _____ les ordures.

EXERCISE D **Le futur.** Ask what each person will do in the future.

EXAMPLE: il/réussir   **Est-ce qu'il réussira?**

1. tu/maigrir

_____

2. je/grossir

_____

3. nous/obéir à nos parents

_____

4. vous/saisir chaque occasion de réussir

_____

5. ils/punir leur frère

_____

6. elle/choisir un bon métier

_____

EXERCISE E **La perte.** Express what the following people will never lose.

EXAMPLE: il /son idéalisme
          Il ne perdra jamais son idéalisme.

1. je / mon sens de l'humour

_____

2. ils / leur sang-froid

_____

3. nous / notre esprit

_____

4. tu / ton appétit

_____

5. vous / votre patience

_____

6. elle / son joli sourire

_____

3.   Spelling Changes in the Future Tense

a. Most verbs with infinitives ending in _–yer_ change _y_ to _i_ in the future.

employer _to use_	
j' emplo*i*erai	nous emplo*i*erons
tu emplo*i*eras	vous emplo*i*erez
il/elle emplo*i*era	ils/elles emplo*i*eront

NOTE: 1.   Verbs with infinitives ending in _–ayer_ may or may not change the _y_ to _i_ in all future-tense forms.

essayer _to try_

j'essaierai (essayerai), tu essaieras (essayeras), il/elle essaiera (essayera), nous essaierons (essayerons), vous essaierez (essayerez), ils essaieront (essayeront).

2.   The verb _envoyer_ is irregular in the future.

envoyer _to send_

j'enverrai, tu enverras, il/elle enverra, nous enverrons, vous enverrez, ils/elles enverront

| EXERCISE F | **Ça m'ennuie.**   Express whom the following people will bother.

EXAMPLE: il/oncle   **Il ennuiera son oncle.**

1. elle/père   _____

2. ils/frère   _____

3. je/mère   _____

4. nous/grands-parents   _____

5. vous/tante   _____

6. tu/sœur   _____

EXERCISE G **Des cadeaux.** Express what each person will send to Hélène as a birthday gift.

EXAMPLE: **Il lui enverra une chemise.**

1. Nous _____.

2. Vous _____.

3. Il _____.

4. Je _____.

5. Tu _____ .

6. Elles _____ .

b. Verbs with silent *e* in the syllable before the infinitive ending change silent *e* to *è* in the future.

acheter *to buy*	
j' achèterai	nous achèterons
tu achèteras	vous achèterez
il/elle achètera	ils/elles achèteront

c. In the future, verbs like *appeler* and *jeter* double the consonant before the infinitive ending.

appeler *to call*	
j' appellerai	nous appellerons
tu appelleras	vous appellerez
il/elle appellera	ils/elles appelleront

jeter *to throw*	
je jetterai	nous jetterons
tu jetteras	vous jetterez
il/elle jettera	ils/elles jetteront

EXERCISE H **La maladie.** Your mother is sick. Say what each family member will do to help her.

EXAMPLE: Jean/achever les travaux ménagers **Jean achèvera** les travaux ménagers

1. nous/acheter les provisions

   _____

2. tu/amener Jacques à l'école

   _____

3. je/promener le chien

   _____

4. mes sœurs/jeter les ordures

   _____

5. mon frère/ appeler le docteur

   _____

6. vous/ ramener Fabienne de l'école

   _____

4.   Verbs Irregular in the Future

The following verbs have irregular stems in the future.

INFINITIVE	FUTURE	INFINITIVE	FUTURE
aller to go	**j'irai**	**pouvoir** to be able to	**je pourrai**
avoir to have	**j'aurai**	**recevoir** to receive	**je recevrai**
envoyer to send	**j'enverrai**	**savoir** to know	**je saurai**
être to be	**je serai**	**venir** to come	**je viendrai**
faire to do	**je ferai**	**voir** to see	**je verrai**
mourir to die	**je mourrai**	**vouloir** to want	**je voudrai**

EXERCISE I   **Les situations.**   Express the three things each person will do in the following situations.

1. Si je gagne le gros lot, je (acheter une nouvelle voiture/aller en France/ faire le tour du monde) _____

   _____

2. Si elle se marie, elle (avoir des enfants/travailler dur/nourrir sa famille)

   _____

   _____

3. S'ils deviennent politiciens, ils (aider les pauvres/protéger l'environnement/être honnêtes)

   _____

   _____

4. Si nous finissons nos études universitaires, nous (recevoir nos diplômes/ devenir célèbres/ pouvoir tout faire) _____

_____

5. Si vous allez en France, vous (voir la Tour Eiffel/envoyer des souvenirs à vos amis/ visiter tous les monuments importants) _____

_____

_____

6. Si tu fais de ton mieux, tu (réussir/être un succès/gagner beaucoup d'argent) _____

_____

EXERCISE J   **Les promesses.**   Express what Henri says he will do if his parents give him permission to study abroad for a year in Paris.

EXAMPLE: étudier beaucoup   **J'étudierai beaucoup.**

1. faire tous mes devoirs   _____

2. envoyer une lettre par semaine   _____

3. mourir de joie   _____

4. être très heureux tout le temps   _____

5. aller à toutes mes classes   _____

6. avoir les meilleures notes de tous   _____

7. recevoir des prix   _____

8. revenir plus sage   _____

9. voir tout ce qu'il y a d'intéressant   _____

10. savoir bien parler la langue française   _____

EXERCISE K   **Le permis de conduire.**   You want to drive your parents' car. Express the questions they are sure to ask you and your negative responses.

EXAMPLE: conduire vite   **Conduiras-tu vite?**
Je ne conduirai pas vite.

1. être impatient(e)   _____

_____

2. faire des bêtises

_____

_____

3. oublier tes responsabilités   _____

_____

4. dire des mensonges

_____

_____

5. avoir des accidents

_____

_____

6. sortir tous les soirs

_____

_____

7. revenir tard

_____

_____

8. aller en ville

_____

_____

EXERCISE L   **Le temps libre.**   Work with a partner. Take turns asking about your plans for this weekend.

_____

_____

_____

_____

_____

EXERCISE M   **Chez une voyante.**   You went to a fortune teller. Write a note to a friend expressing what was predicted for your future.

_____

_____

_____

_____

_____

Appendix

1. Verbs With Regular Forms

INFINITIVE

danser	finir	rendre	se laver

PAST PARTICIPLE

dansé	fini	rendu	lavé

PRESENT

danse	finis	rends	me lave
danses	finis	rends	te laves
danse	finit	rend	se lave
dansons	finissons	rendons	nous lavons
dansez	finissez	rendez	vous lavez
dansent	finissent	rendent	se lavent

IMPERATIVE

danse	finis	rends	lave-toi
dansons	finissons	rendons	lavons-nous
dansez	finissez	rendez	lavez-vous

IMPERFECT

dansais	finissais	rendais	me lavais
dansais	finissais	rendais	te lavais
dansait	finisssait	rendait	se lavait
dansions	finissions	rendions	nous lavions
dansiez	finissiez	rendiez	vous laviez
dansaient	finissaient	rendaient	se lavaient

FUTURE

danserai	finirai	rendrai	me laverai
danseras	finiras	rendras	te laveras
dansera	finira	rendra	se lavera
danserons	finirons	rendrons	nous laverons
danserez	finirez	rendrez	vous laverez
danseront	finiront	rendront	se laveront

PASSÉ COMPOSÉ

ai dansé	ai fini	ai rendu	**me** suis lavé(e)
as dansé	as fini	as rendu	**t'**es lavé(e)
a dansé	a fini	a rendu	**s'**est lavé(e)
avons dansé	avons fini	avons rendu	**nous** sommes lavé(e)s
avez dansé	avez fini	avez rendu	**vous** êtes lavé(e)(s)
ont dansé	ont fini	ont rendu	**se** sont lavé(e)s

2. –*er* Verbs With Spelling Changes

	-*cer* VERBS	-*ger* VERBS	-*yer* VERBS*	-*eler* / -*eter* VERBS		e + CONSONANT + -*er* VERBS	é + CONSONANT(S) + -*er* VERBS
INFINITIVE	lan**cer**	na**ger**	ennu**yer**	app**eler**	j**eter**	l**e**ver	rép**éter**
PRESENT	lance	nage	**ennuie**	**appelle**	**jette**	**lève**	**répète**
	lances	nages	**ennuies**	**appelles**	**jettes**	**lèves**	**répètes**
	lance	nage	**ennuie**	**appelle**	**jette**	**lève**	**répète**
	lançons	**nageons**	ennuyons	appelons	jetons	levons	répétons
	lancez	nagez	ennuyez	appelez	jetez	levez	répétez
	lancent	nagent	**ennuient**	**appellent**	**jettent**	**lèvent**	**répètent**
IMPERFECT	**lançais**	**nageais**					
	lançais	**nageais**					
	lançait	**nageait**					
	lancions	nagions					
	lanciez	nagiez					
	lançaient	**nageaient**					
FUTURE			**ennuierai**	**appellerai**	**jetterai**	**lèverai**	
			ennuieras	**appelleras**	**jetteras**	**lèveras**	
			ennuiera	**appellera**	**jettera**	**lèvera**	
			ennuierons	**appellerons**	**jetterons**	**lèverons**	
			ennuierez	**appellerez**	**jetterez**	**lèverez**	
			ennuieront	**appelleront**	**jetteront**	**lèveront**	
IMPERATIVE	lance	nage	**ennuie**	**appelle**	**jette**	**lève**	**répète**
	lançons	**nageons**	ennuyons	appelons	jetons	levons	répétons
	lancez	nagez	ennuyez	appelez	jetez	levez	répétez

* Verbs ending in *-ayer*, like *payer* and *essayer,* may be conjugated like *ennuyer* or retain the *y* in all conjugations: *j'essaie* or *j'essaye.*

3. Verbs With Irregular Forms

NOTE: 1. Irregular forms are printed in bold type.

2. Verbs conjugated with *être* in compound tenses are indicated with an asterisk (*)

INFINITIVE, PARTICIPLE	PRESENT	IMPERATIVE	IMPERFECT	FUTURE	PASSÉ COMPOSÉ
aller* *to go*	**vais**	va	allais	**irai**	suis allé(e)
	vas	allons	allais	**iras**	es allé(e)
	va	allez	allait	**ira**	est allé(e)
allé	allons		allions	**irons**	sommes allé(e)s
	allez		alliez	**irez**	êtes allé(e)(s)
	vont		allaient	**iront**	sont allé(e)s

apprendre *to learn* (like **prendre**)

avoir	**ai**	**aie**	avais	**aurai**	ai **eu**
to have	**as**	**ayons**	avais	**auras**	as **eu**
	a	**ayez**	avait	**aura**	a **eu**
eu	**avons**		avions	**aurons**	avons **eu**
	avez		aviez	**aurez**	avez **eu**
	ont		avaient	**auront**	ont **eu**

comprendre *to understand* (like **prendre**)

découvir *to discover* (like **couvrir**)

devenir* *to become* (like **venir**)

dire	dis	dis	disais	**dirai**	ai **dit**
to say, to tell	dis	disons	disais	**diras**	as **dit**
	dit	dites	disait	**dira**	a **dit**
dit	**disons**		disions	**dirons**	avons **dit**
	dites		disiez	**direz**	avez **dit**
	disent		disaient	**diront**	ont **dit**

écrire	écris	écris	écrivais	écrirai	ai **écrit**
to write	écris	écrivons	écrivais	écriras	as **écrit**
	écrit	écrivez	écrivait	écrira	a **écrit**
écrit	**écrivons**		écrivions	écrirons	avons **écrit**
	écrivez		écriviez	écrirez	avez **écrit**
	écrivent		écrivaient	écriront	ont **écrit**

INFINITIVE, PARTICIPLE	PRESENT	IMPERATIVE	IMPERFECT	FUTURE	PASSÉ COMPOSÉ
envoyer *to send* **envoyé**	**envoie** **envoies** **envoie** envoyons envoyez **envoient**	envoie envoyons envoyez	envoyais envoyais envoyait envoyions envoyiez envoyaient	**enverrai** **enverras** **enverra** **enverrons** **enverrez** **enverront**	ai envoyé as envoyé a envoyé avons envoyé avez envoyé ont envoyé
être *to be* **été**	**suis** es est **sommes** **êtes** **sont**	**sois** **soyons** **soyez**	**étais** **étais** **était** **étions** **étiez** **étaient**	**serai** seras sera serons serez seront	ai **été** as **été** a **été** avons **été** avez **été** ont **été**
faire *to do, to make* **fait**	fais fais **fait** **faisons** **faites** **font**	fais faisons faites	faisais faisais faisait faisions faisiez faisaient	**ferai** **feras** **fera** **ferons** **ferez** **feront**	ai **fait** as **fait** a **fait** avons **fait** avez **fait** ont **fait**
lire *to read* **lu**	lis lis **lit** **lisons** **lisez** **lisent**	lis lisons lisez	lisais lisais lisait lisions lisiez lisaient	lirai liras lira lirons lirez liront	ai **lu** as **lu** a **lu** avons **lu** avez **lu** ont **lu**
mettre *to put* **mis**	**mets** **mets** **met** mettons mettez mettent	mets mettons mettez	mettais mettais mettait mettions mettiez mettaient	mettrai mettras mettra mettrons mettrez mettront	ai **mis** as **mis** a **mis** avons **mis** avez **mis** ont **mis**
ouvrir *to open* **ouvert**	**ouvre** **ouvres** **ouvre** **ouvrons** **ouvrez** **ouvrent**	**ouvre** ouvrons ouvrez	ouvrais ouvrais ouvrait ouvrions ouvriez ouvraient	ouvrirai ouvriras ouvrira ouvrirons ouvrirez ouvriront	ai **ouvert** as **ouvert** a **ouvert** avons **ouvert** avez **ouvert** ont **ouvert**

INFINITIVE, PARTICIPLE	PRESENT	IMPERATIVE	IMPERFECT	FUTURE	PASSÉ COMPOSÉ

partir* *to leave* (like **sortir**)

permettre *to allow* (like **mettre**)

INFINITIVE, PARTICIPLE	PRESENT	IMPERATIVE	IMPERFECT	FUTURE	PASSÉ COMPOSÉ
pouvoir *to be able* **pu**	**peux (puis)** **peux** **peut** **pouvons** **pouvez** **peuvent**		pouvais pouvais pouvait pouvions pouviez pouvaient	**pourrai** **pourras** **pourra** **pourrons** **pourrez** **pourront**	ai **pu** as **pu** a **pu** avons **pu** avez **pu** ont **pu**
prendre *to take* **pris**	prends prends prend **prenons** **prenez** **prennent**	prends prenons prenez	prenais prenais prenait prenions preniez prenaient	prendrai prendras prendra prendrons prendrez prendront	ai **pris** as **pris** a **pris** avons **pris** avez **pris** ont **pris**

promettre *to promise* (like **mettre**)

INFINITIVE, PARTICIPLE	PRESENT	IMPERATIVE	IMPERFECT	FUTURE	PASSÉ COMPOSÉ
recevoir *to receive* **reçu**	**reçois** **reçois** **reçoit** **recevons** **recevez** **reçoivent**	reçois recevons recevez	recevais recevais recevait recevions receviez recevaient	**recevrai** **recevras** **recevra** **recevrons** **recevrez** **recevront**	ai **reçu** as **reçu** a **reçu** avons **reçu** avez **reçu** ont **reçu**
savoir *to know* *(how to)* **su**	**sais** **sais** **sait** **savons** **savez** **savent**	**sache** **sachons** **sachez**	savais savais savait savions saviez savaient	**saurai** **sauras** **saura** **saurons** **saurez** **sauront**	ai **su** as **su** a **su** avons **su** avez **su** ont **su**
sortir* *to go out* **sorti**	**sors** **sors** **sort** **sortons** **sortez** **sortent**	sors sortons sortez	sortais sortais sortait sortions sortiez sortaient	sortirai sortiras sortira sortirons sortirez sortiront	suis sorti(e) es sorti(e) est sorti(e) sommes sorti(e)s êtes sorti(e)(s) sont sorti(e)s

INFINITIVE, PARTICIPLE	PRESENT	IMPERATIVE	IMPERFECT	FUTURE	PASSÉ COMPOSÉ
venir* *to come* **venu**	**viens** **viens** **vient** **venons** **venez** **viennent**	viens venons venez	venais venais venait venions veniez venaient	**viendrai** **viendras** **viendra** **viendrons** **viendrez** **viendront**	suis **venu(e)** es **venu(e)** est **venu(e)** sommes **venu(e)s** êtes **venu(e)(s)** sont **venu(e)s**
voir *to see* **vu**	**vois** **vois** **voit** **voyons** **voyez** **voient**	vois voyons voyez	voyais voyais voyait voyions voyiez voyaient	**verrai** **verras** **verra** **verrons** **verrez** **verront**	ai **vu** as **vu** a **vu** avons **vu** avez **vu** ont **vu**
vouloir *to want* **voulu**	**veux** **veux** **veut** voulons voulez **veulent**	**veuille** **veuillons** **veuillez**	voulais voulais voulait voulions vouliez voulaient	**voudrai** **voudras** **voudra** **voudrons** **voudrez** **voudront**	ai **voulu** as **voulu** a **voulu** avons **voulu** avez **voulu** ont **voulu**

4. Common Reflexive Verbs

s'acheter *to buy for oneself*
s'amuser (à) *to have a good time, enjoy*
s'appeler *to be named*
se brosser *to brush oneself*
se coucher *to lie down; to go to bed*
se demander *to wonder*
se dépêcher (de) *to hurry*
se déshabiller *to undress*
s'ennuyer (à) *to get bored*
s'habiller *to dress*
se laver *to wash oneself*

se lever *to get up; to rise*
se maquiller *to put on makeup*
se marier (avec) *to get married (to)*
se mettre en route *to start out*
se peigner *to comb one's hair*
se préparer *to prepare oneself*
se promener *to take a walk*
se rappeler *to remember*
se raser *to shave*
se reposer *to rest*
se réveiller *to wake up*

5. Common Prepositions

a. Simple Prepositions

à *to, at, in*
après *after*
avant *before*

avec *with*
chez *to/at, in the house (place) of (a person)*
contre *against*

dans	*in, into, within*	**pour**	*for*
de	*of , from*	**sans**	*without*
depuis	*since, for*	**sauf**	*except*
derrière	*behind*	**selon**	*according to*
devant	*in front of*	**sous**	*under*
en	*in, into, as*	**sur**	*on*
entre	*among, between*	**vers**	*toward*
par	*by, through*		

b. Compound Prepositions

à cause de	*because of, on account of*	**autour de**	*around*
à côté de	*next to, beside*	**avant (de)**	*before*
à droite de	*on (to) the right*	**du côté de**	*in the direction of, near*
à gauche de	*on (to) the left*	**en face de**	*opposite*
au lieu de	*instead of*	**loin de**	*far from*
au milieu de	*in the middle of*	**près de**	*near*

6. Punctuation

French punctuation, though similar to English, has the following major differences:

(a) The comma is not used before *et* or *ou* in a series.

Elle a acheté la robe, la jupe et la chemise.	*She bought the dress, the skirt, and the shirt.*

(b) In numbers, French uses a comma where English uses a period and a period (decimal point) where English uses a comma.

1.900 (mille neuf cent)	*1,900 (one thousand nine hundred)*
9,15 (neuf virgule quinze)	*9.15 (nine point one five)*

(c) French closing quotation marks, unlike English, precede the comma or period; however, the quotation mark follows a period if the quotation mark encloses a completed statement.

Il demande: «Est-ce que tu as faim?»	*He asks: "Are you hungry?"*
«Non», répond-elle.	*"No," she answers.*

7. Syllabication

French words are generally divided at the end of a line according to units of sound or syllables. A French syllable generally begins with a consonant and ends with a vowel.

(a) If a single consonant comes between two vowels, the division is made before the consonant.

pa-**ti**-ner   ré-**pond**   cha-**peau**

NOTE: A division cannot be made either before or after *x* or *y* when *x* or *y* come between two vowels.

exact   **tuyau**

(b) If two consonants are combined between two vowels, the division is made between the two consonants.

e**s**-prit   da**n-s**er

NOTE: If the second consonant is *r* or *l,* the division is made before the two consonants.

ca-pa-**ble**   pren-**dre**

(c) If three or more consonants are combined between vowels, the division is made after the second consonant.

co**mp-t**er   i**ns-t**aller

(d) Two vowels may not be divided.

na-**tio**n   th**éâ**-tre

French-English Vocabulary

The French-English vocabulary is intended to be complete for the context of this book. Irregular noun plurals are given in full: **œil** *(m.)* *(pl.* **yeux***).* Irregular feminine of adjectives are also given in full: **beau***(f.* **belle***).* Regular feminine forms are indicated by **(e),** or the consonant that is doubled before adding e: **bon(ne)**, or the ending that replaces the masculine ending: **baigneur (-euse).**

An asterisk (*) indicates an aspirate **h**: **la honte, le haricot.**

ABBREVIATIONS

(adj.)	adjective	*(m.)*	masculine
(adv.)	adverb	*(m./f.)*	masculine or feminine
(coll.)	colloquial	*(pl.)*	plural
(inf.)	infinitive	*(p.p.)*	past participle
(f.)	feminine		

à at, to; **à bientôt** see you soon; **à cause de** because of; **à côté (de)** next (to); **à demain** see you tomorrow; **à droite (de)** to the right (of); **à gauche (de)** to the left (of); **à l'avance** in advance; **à l'heure** on time; **à partir de** from; **à peu près** about, approximately; **à pied** on foot; **à tout à l'heure** see you later: **à travers** across, through

abord: d'abord at first

accompagner to accompany

accomplissement *(m.)* accomplishment

acheter to buy

achever to complete, to finish

acteur *(m.)* actor

actif (-ive) active

actrice *(f.)* actress

admirer to admire

adorer to adore

aéroport *(m.)* airport

affaire *(f.)* affair; **affaires** *(f. pl.)* business; things

âgé(e) old

agent de police *(m.)* police officer

agréable agreeable, nice

aider to help

aimable friendly, kind

aimer to like, to love; **aimer mieux** to prefer

algèbre *(f.)* algebra

Allemagne *(f.)* Germany

aller to go; **aller à la pêche** to go fishing; **aller à pied** to walk, to go on foot; **aller bien** to feel well; **aller en voiture** to go by car; **aller mal** to feel poorly

allumer to light, to turn on

alors then, thus, so

ambitieux (-euse) ambitious

amener to bring; to lead to

ami(e) friend; **petit ami** boyfriend; **petite amie** girlfriend

amitié *(f.)* friendship

amour *(m.)* love

amoureux (-euse) in love

amusant(e) fun, amusing

amusement *(m.)* fun

amuser to amuse; **s'amuser** to have a good time, to have fun

an *(m.)* year; **avoir... ans** to be . . . years old

ancien(ne) old, ancient, former

anglais(e) English

Angleterre *(f.)* England

animal *(m.)* *(pl.* **-aux***)* animal

année *(f.)* year

anniversaire *(m.)* birthday; **bon anniversaire** happy birthday

annonce *(f.)* advertisement; announcement; **annonce publicitaire** advertisement; **petite annonce** classified ad.

anxieux (-euse) anxious

août *(m.)* August

appartement *(m.)* apartment

appeler to call; **s'appeler** to be named, call oneself

applaudir to applaud

apporter to bring

apprécier to appreciate

apprendre *(p.p.* **appris***)* to learn; **apprendre (à)** to learn; to teach

après after, afterward; **après tout** after all; **d'après** based upon

après-midi (*m.*) afternoon

arbre (*m.*) tree

argent (*m.*) money; silver

armoire (*f.*) wardrobe

arrêter to stop; to arrest; **s'arrêter (de)** to stop

arriver to arrive, to come; to happen

artiste (*m./f.*) artist

ascenseur (*m.*) elevator

aspirateur (*m.*) vacuum cleaner; **passer l'aspirateur** to vacuum

assez enough; rather; **assez (de)** enough (of)

assiette (*f.*) plate

assis(e) seated

assister (à) to assist; to attend

attendre to wait (for)

attentif (-ive) attentive

attention (*f.*) attention; **faire attention (à)** to pay attention (to)

attraction (*f.*) attraction; **parc d'attractions** amusement park

au (*pl.* aux) at the, to the; **au bas de** at the bottom of; **au contraire** on the contrary; **au fond (de)** in/at the bottom (of); **au haut (de)** in/at the top (of); **au lieu de** instead of; **au milieu de** in the middle of; **au moins** at least; **au revoir** goodbye

aujourd'hui today

aussi also, too; as

auteur (*m.*) author

auto (*f.*) car; **en auto** by car

autobus (*m.*) bus

automne (*m.*) fall, autumn

autour (de) around

autre other; another

autrefois formerly

avancer to advance; **à l'avance** in advance

avant (de) before

avant-hier the day before yesterday

avec with

aveugle blind

avion (*m.*) airplane; **en avion** by airplane

avocat(e) lawyer

avoir to have (*p.p.* **eu**); **avoir... ans** to be . . . years old; **avoir besoin (de)** to need; **avoir chaud** to be hot (*of persons*); **avoir envie de** to desire, to want, to feel like; **avoir faim** to be hungry; **avoir froid** to be cold (*of persons*); **avoir honte (de)** to be ashamed (of); **avoir l'air (de)** to appear, to seem; **avoir l'habitude de** to be accustomed to, to be in the habit of; **avoir (de) la chance** to be lucky; **avoir le temps (de)** to have the time (to); **avoir mal à** to have an ache in; **avoir peur (de)** to be afraid (of); **avoir raison** to be right; **avoir soif** to be thirsty; **avoir sommeil** to be sleepy; **avoir tort** to be wrong

avril (*m.*) April

bain (*m.*) bath; **maillot de bain** (*m.*) bathing suit; **salle de bains** (*f.*) bathroom

baladeur (*m.*) portable cassette player, Walkman

balle (*f.*) ball

banane (*f.*) banana

banc (*m.*) seat, bench

bande (*f.*) band, strip; **bande dessinée** comic strip, comic book

banque (*f.*) bank

bas(se) low; **en bas** downstairs; **en bas (de)** at the bottom (of)

basket (*f.*) basketball sneaker

basket (*m.*) basketball

bateau (*m.*) (*pl.* **-aux**) boat

bâtiment (*m.*) building

bâtir to build

bâton (*m.*) stick; pole

bavarder to chat

beau, bel (*f.* **belle**) beautiful, handsome; **faire beau** to be beautiful (*weather*);

beaucoup (de) a lot (of), many, much

beauté (*f.*) beauty

bébé (*m.*) baby

besoin (*m.*) need; **avoir besoin de** to need

beurre (*m.*) butter

bibliothèque (*f.*) library

bicyclette (*f.*) bicycle; **monter à bicyclette** to go bicycle riding

bien well; **aller bien** to feel well; **bien sûr** of course

bientôt soon; **à bientôt** see you soon

bifteck (*m.*) steak

bijou (*m.*) jewel

billet (*m.*) bill; ticket

biologie (*f.*) biology

bise (*f.*) (*coll.*) kiss; **grosses bises** lots of love

blanc(he) white; **blanc** (*m.*) egg white

bleu(e) blue

blouse (*f.*) blouse

bœuf (*m.*) beef

boire (*p.p.* **bu**) to drink

bois wood (*m.*)

boisson (*f.*) drink

boîte (*f.*) box, can; **bol** (*m.*) bowl

bon(ne) good; **bon anniversaire** happy birthday;

bon marché inexpensive;
bonne année happy new
year; **bonne chance** good
luck; **de bonne heure** early
bonbon (*m.*) candy
bonheur (*m.*) happiness
bonhomme (*m.*) chap;
bonhomme de neige
snowman
bonjour hello
bord (*m.*) edge;
à bord on board
botte (*f.*) boot
bouche (*f.*) mouth
boucher (-ère) butcher
boucherie (*f.*) butcher shop
bouger to move
bouillabaisse (*f.*) fish stew
boulanger (-ère) baker
boulangerie (*f.*) bakery
boule (*f.*) ball; **boule de neige**
snowball
boum (*f.*) party
bouteille (*f.*) bottle
bracelet (*m.*) bracelet
bras (*m.*) arm
brosser to brush; **se brosser** to
brush oneself
bruit (*m.*) noise
brun(e) brown, brunette
bureau (*m.*) desk; office;
bureau de poste (*m.*) post
office

ça that; **ça ne fait rien** it
doesn't matter
cadeau (*m.*) gift, present
café (*m.*) coffee; café
cahier (*m.*) notebook
caissier (-ière) cashier
calculette (*f.*) calculator
calendrier (*m.*) calendar
campagne (*f.*) country
canapé (*m.*) sofa
car because
car (*m.*) tour bus
carotte (*f.*) carrot

cartable (*m.*) school bag
carte (*f.*) card; map; **carte de
crédit** credit card; **carte
postale** postcard
carton (*m.*) carton, cardboard
cas (*m.*) case;
en cas de in case of
casser to break
cathédrale (*f.*) cathedral
cause (*f.*) cause; **à cause de**
because of
ce it, he, she, they; this, that;
ce que that which, what
céder to yield
cela that
célèbre famous
célébrer to celebrate
cent (one) hundred
centre (*m.*) center; **centre
commercial** shopping mall
cercle (*m.*) club
céréales (*f. pl.*) cereal
cerise (*f.*) cherry
certain(e) certain, sure
ces these, those
cesser to stop
cet(te) this, that
chacun(e) each one
chaîne: chaîne stéréo (*f.*)
stereo; **chaîne de montagnes**
mountain range
chaise (*f.*) chair
chambre (à coucher) (*f.*)
bedroom
champ (*m.*) field
chance (*f.*) luck; **avoir (de) la
chance** to be lucky; **bonne
chance** good luck
chanson (*f.*) song
chanter to sing
chanteur (-euse) singer
chapeau (*m.*) (*pl.* **-aux**) hat
chaque each
charcuterie (*f.*) delicatessen
charmant(e) charming
chat(te) cat
château (*m.*) (*pl.* **-aux**) castle

chaud(e) warm, hot; **avoir
chaud** to be hot (*of persons*);
faire chaud to be warm/hot
(*weather*)
chauffer to heat, to warm
chaussette (*f.*) sock
chaussure (*f.*) shoe
chef (*m.*) chef, cook, chief, head
chemin (*m.*) road; **chemin de
fer** (*m.*) railroad
cheminée (*f.*) fireplace
chemise (*f.*) shirt
chemisier (*m.*) woman's shirt
chèque (*m.*) check; **chèque de
voyage** traveler's check
cher (-ère) dear; expensive
chercher to look for, to search
cheval (*m.*) (*pl.* **-aux**) horse
cheveu (*m.*) (*pl.* **-eux**) hair
(*one strand*)
chez to/at (the house/place of)
chien(ne) dog
chiffre (*m.*) number
chimie (*f.*) chemistry
chocolat (*m.*) chocolate; hot
chocolate; **mousse au chocolat**
(*f.*) chocolate mousse
choisir to choose
choix (*m.*) choice
chose (*f.*) thing
ciel (*m.*) heaven, sky
cinéma (*m.*) movies
cinq five
cinquante fifty
circonstance (*f.*) circumstance
cirque (*m.*) circus
ciseaux (*m. pl.*) scissors
citoyen(ne) citizen
citron (*m.*) lemon
classe (*f.*) classe; **classe de
neige** snow class; **salle de
classe** classroom (*f.*)
classeur (*m.*) looseleaf notebook
clef (*f.*) key
climat (*m.*) climate
cloche (*f.*) bell
cochon (*m.*) pig

cœur (*m.*) heart
coiffeur (-euse) hairdresser
coin (*m.*) corner
collège (*m.*) secondary school
collier (*m.*) necklace
colonie (*f.*) colony; colonie de
  vacances camp
combien (de) how many, much
commander to order
comme as, like
commencer to begin
comment how
commérages (*m. pl.*) gossip
compagnie (*f.*) company
compléter to complete
comprendre (*p.p.* compris) to
  understand
compter to count; to intend
concert (*m.*) concert
conducteur (*f.* -trice) driver
conduire (*p.p.* conduit) to
  drive; permis (*m.*) de
  conduire driver's license
connaissance (*f.*) acquaintance,
  knowledge; faire la
  connaissance (de) to make
  the acquaintance of
connaître (*p.p.* connu) to
  know, to be acquainted with
consciencieux (-euse)
  conscientious
conseiller to advise
construire (*p.p.* construit) to
  construct, to build
contagieux (-euse) contagious
contraire (*m.*) opposite;
  au contraire on the contrary
contre against
convenir to fit
copain (*f.* copine) friend, pal
copier to copy
corps (*m.*) body
correspondant(e) pen pal
correspondre to correspond;
  to exchange letters
corriger to correct
costume (*m.*) costume; suit

côté (*m.*) side; à côté (de) next
  (to); de côté aside; de l'autre
  côté on the other side
cou (*m.*) neck
coucher to put to bed;
  se coucher to go to bed
couleur (*f.*) color
coup (*m.*) blow; coup de main
  helping hand
couper to cut
courage (*m.*) courage
courir (*p.p.* couru) to run
courrier (*m.*) mail
cours (*m.*) course, subject
course (*f.*) errand; race ; faire
  des courses to go shopping
court(e) short
couteau (*m.*) knife
coûter to cost; coûter cher to
  be expensive
couvert (*m.*) cover; mettre le
  couvert to set the table
couvrir (*p.p.* couvert) to cover;
  se couvrir to cover oneself
craie (*f.*) chalk; bâton de craie
  (*m.*) stick of chalk
cravate (*f.*) tie
crayon (*m.*) pencil
crier to shout
critiquer to criticize
croire to believe
croix (*f.*) cross
cuiller (*f.*) spoon
cuire (*p.p.* cuit) to cook
cuisine (*f.*) kitchen; cooking;
  faire la cuisine to cook
cuisiner to cook

d'abord first, at first
d'accord okay; all right?
d'habitude usually
dangereux (-euse) dangerous
dans, in, into, within
danser to dance
date (*f.*) date; date limite
  deadline
davantage more

de of, about, from; d'abord at
  first; d'après based upon; de
  bonne heure early; de côté
  aside; de l'autre côté on the
  other side; de long en large
  back and forth; de nouveau
  again; de rien you're
  welcome; de temps en
  temps from time to time
débarrasser to clear
debout standing; up
décembre December
décider to decide
découvrir (*p.p.* découvert)
  to discover
décrire (*p.p.* décrit) to describe
dedans inside
défendre to defend; to forbid
dehors outside
déjà already
déjeuner (*m.*) lunch; to eat
  lunch
délicieux (-euse) delicious
demain tomorrow; à demain
  see you tomorrow
demander to ask (for)
déménager to move (*to another
  residence*)
demi(e) half; demi-heure (*f.*)
  half hour
dent (*f.*) tooth; brosse à dents
  tooth brush
dentiste (*m./f.*) dentist
dépêcher to dispatch;
  se dépêcher to hurry
dépenser to spend (*money*)
depuis for, since
déranger to bother, disturb
dernier (-ière) last
derrière behind
des some; of the; from the;
  about the
descendre to go down; to take
  down
déshabiller to undress; se
  déshabiller to get undressed
désirer to desire, to want

désobéir (à) to disobey

dessert (*m.*) dessert

dessin (*m.*) drawing, design; **dessin animé** cartoon

dessiner to draw

détester to hate

deux two

deuxième second

devant in front (of)

devenir (*p.p.* **devenu**) to become

devoirs (*m. pl.*) homework

dictionnaire (*m.*) dictionary

difficile difficult

diligent(e) hard working

dimanche (*m.*) Sunday

dîner (*m.*) dinner

dîner to dine, eat dinner

dire (*p.p.* **dit**) to say, to tell

directeur (*f.* **directrice**) director, principal

diriger to direct

discuter (de) to discuss

dispute (*f.*) quarrel

disque (*m.*) record; **disque compact** compact disc, CD; **disque vidéo** laser disc

divan (*m.*) day bed

diviser to divide

divisé(e) divided; **divisé par** divided by

dix ten

dix-huit eighteen

dix-neuf nineteen

dix-sept seventeen

docteur (*m.*) doctor

doigt (*m.*) finger

dollar (*m.*) dollar

donc therefore

donner to give

dormir to sleep

dos (*m.*) back; **sac à dos** backpack

d'où from where

doute (*m.*) doubt; **sans doute** without a doubt

doux (*f.* **douce**) sweet, mild, gentle

douzaine (*f.*) dozen

douze twelve

drapeau (*m.*) flag

droit (*m.*) right

droit(e) right; **tout droit** straight ahead

drôle funny; strange

du some, any; of the

dur(e) hard

durer to last

eau (*f.*) water; **eau minérale** mineral water

écharpe (*f.*) scarf

échecs (*m. pl.*) chess

éclairer to light

école (*f.*) school; **faire l'école buissonnière** to cut classes, play hookey

écouter to listen (to)

écrire (*p.p.* **écrit**) to write; **machine à écrire** (*f.*) typewriter

écrivain (*m.*) writer

édifice (*m.*) building

éditeur (*f.* **éditrice**) editor

effacer to erase

église (*f.*) church

égoïste selfish

éléphant (*m.*) elephant

élève (*m./f.*) pupil; student

élever to bring up, to raise

elle, she, it, her

elles they, them

embrasser to kiss

émission (*f.*) program

emmener to take away, lead away

empêcher (de) to prevent (from)

emploi (*m.*) job; **emploi du temps** (*m.*) schedule, program

employer to use

emprunter (à) to borrow (from)

en in; to ; **en auto** by car; **en avion** by airplane; **en bas** downstairs, **en bas (de)** at the bottom (of); **en cas de** in case of; **en face (de)** opposite; **en haut** upstairs; **en place** in place; **en retard** late; **en train de** in the middle of; **en ville** downtown

en about it/them, from it/them, of it/them; from there

encore still, yet, again

encre (*f.*) ink

endroit (*m.*) place

enfant (*m./f.*) child

enfin at last, finally

enlever to remove, to take off

ennui (*m.*) boredom, problem

ennuyer to bore; to bother; **s'ennuyer** to become bored

ennuyeux (-euse) annoying, boring

énormément enormously, a great deal

enseigner to teach

ensemble together

ensuite then

entendre to hear

entier(-ère) entire, whole

entraîneur (*m.*) coach

entre between, among

entrée (*f.*) entrance

entrer to enter, to go in

enveloppe (*f.*) envelope

envie (*f.*) desire, want; **avoir envie (de)** to desire, to want; to feel like

environnement (*m.*) environment

envoyer to send

épaule (*f.*) shoulder

épicier (-ière) grocer

épicerie (*f.*) grocery store

épouser to marry

équipe (*f.*) team

équipement (*m.*) equipment

erreur (*f.*) error, mistake
escalier (*m.*) staircase
espace (*m.*) space
espagnol(e) Spanish
espérer to hope
esprit (*m.*) spirit, mind
essai (*m.*) essay
essayer (de) to try (to)
essence (*f.*) gasoline
essuyer to wipe
est (*m.*) east
estimer to hold in esteem
estomac (*m.*) stomach
et and, plus
étage (*m.*) floor, story
étagère (*f.*) shelf
état (*m.*) state; **États-Unis**
  (*m. pl.*) United States
été (*m.*) summer; **en été** in the
  summer
étoile (*f.*) star
étrange strange
étranger (-ère) foreign
étranger (-ère) foreigner;
  à l'étranger abroad
être (*p.p.* **été**) to be; **être à** to
  belong to; **être en train de** to
  be (in the act of) doing
  something
étude (*f.*) study
étudiant(e) student
étudier to study
eux they, them
événement (*m.*) event
examen (*m.*) test
exemple (*m.*) example;
  par exemple for example
exercice (*m.*) exercise
expérience (*f.*) experience,
  experiment
explication (*f.*) explanation
expliquer to explain
explorer to explore
exprimer to express

fabriquer to manufacture

fâché(e) angry
facile easy
façon (*f.*) fashion, way, manner;
  de cette façon this way
facteur(-trice) mail carrier
faible weak
faim (*f.*) hunger; **avoir faim**
  to be hungry
faire (*p.p.* **fait**) to make, do;
  faire attention (à) to pay
  attention (to); **faire beau** to
  be beautiful (*weather*); **faire
  chaud** to be warm/hot
  (*weather*); **faire de son
  mieux** to do one's best; **faire
  des courses** to go shopping;
  faire du camping to go
  camping; **faire du karaté** to
  do karate; **faire du patin à
  glace** to go ice skating; **faire
  du soleil** to be sunny; **faire
  du sport** to play sports; **faire
  du surf** to go surfing; **faire
  du vent** to be windy; **faire
  fortune** to make a fortune;
  faire frais to be cool
  (*weather*); **faire froid** to be
  cold (*weather*); **faire (la)
  connaissance (de)** to make
  the acquaintance (of); **faire
  la cuisine** to cook; **faire la
  vaisselle** to do the dishes;
  faire le lit to make the bed;
  faire le ménage to do the
  housework; **faire mauvais**
  to be bad (*weather*) **faire
  partie de** to belong to; **faire
  plaisir (à)** to please; **faire
  un voyage** to take a trip;
  faire une promenade to go
  for a walk
famille (*f.*) family; **en famille**
  with the family
fatigué(e) tired
faute (*f.*) mistake
fauteuil (*m.*) armchair

faux, (*f.* **fausse**) false
femme (*f.*) woman, wife;
  femme de ménage cleaning
  woman
fenêtre (*f.*) window
férié(e): jour férié legal
  holiday
ferme (*f.*) farm
fermer to close
fermier (-ière) farmer
fête (*f.*) feast, holiday, party
feu (*m.*) fire; **feu d'artifice**
  fireworks
feuille (*f.*) leaf
février (*m.*) February
fidèle faithful
fier (*f.* **fière**) proud
fièvre (*f.*) fever
figure (*f.*) face
fille (*f.*) daughter, girl
film (*m.*) movie; **film vidéo**
  video tape
fils (*m.*) son; **petit-fils** (*m.*)
  grandson
fin (*f.*) end
finalement finally
finir to finish
fleur (*f.*) flower
fleuve (*m.*) river
fois (*f.*) time (*in a series*);
  trois fois three times;
  à la fois at the same time
fond (*m.*) bottom; **au fond (de)**
  at the bottom (of)
font equals; *see faire*
football (*m.*) (*coll.* **foot**) soccer;
  football américain (*m.*)
  football
force (*f.*) strength; force
forêt (*f.*) forest
forme (*f.*) form
formidable great
formulaire (*m.*) form
fort(e) strong; loud (*voice*)
four (*m.*) oven
fourchette (*f.*) fork

frais, (*f.* **fraîche**) fresh, cool;
  faire frais to be cool weather
fraise (*f.*) strawberry
franc(he) frank
français(e) French
frapper to knock
frère (*m.*) brother
frites (*f. pl.*) French fries
froid(e), froid (*m.*) cold; **avoir
  froid** to be cold (*of persons*);
  faire froid to be cold (*weather*)
fromage (*m.*) cheese
fruit (*m.*) fruit; **fruits de mer**
  (*m. pl.*) seafood
fruiterie (*f.*) fruit store
furieux (-euse) furious

gagner to win; to earn
gant (*m.*) glove
garage (*m.*) garage
garçon (*m.*) boy; waiter
garder to keep; to take care of
gare (*f.*) train station
gâteau (*m.*) cake; **gâteau au
  chocolat** chocolate cake
gâter to spoil
gauche left
geler to freeze
général (pl **-aux**) general
généreux (-euse) generous
gens (*m. pl.*) people
gentil(le) kind, nice
gentiment gently
géographie (*f.*) geography
glace (*f.*) ice; ice cream; mirror
golf (*m.*) golf
gomme (*f.*) eraser
gorge (*f.*) throat
goûter to taste
goûter (*m.*) snack
gracieux (-euse) graceful
grammaire (*f.*) grammar
grand(e) large, big; tall
grand-mère (*f.*) grandmother
grand-parent (*m.*) grandparent
grand-père (*m.*) grandfather
grandir to grow

grenier (*m.*) attic
grippe (*f.*) flu
gris(e) gray
gronder to scold
gros(se) big; fat
grossir to become fat
groupe (*m.*) group
guérir to cure
guichet (*m.*) ticket window
guide (*m.*) guide
guitare (*f.*) guitar
gymnase (*m.*) gymnasium
gymnastique (*f.*) gym,
  gymnastics

habiller to dress; **s'habiller**
  to get dressed
habitant(e) inhabitant
habiter to live (in)
habits (*m. pl.*) clothes
habitude (*f.*) habit; **avoir
  l'habitude de** to be
  accustomed to, to be in the
  habit of; **d'habitude** usually
*****hamburger** (*m.*) hamburger
*****haricot** (*m.*) bean; *****haricots
  verts** (*m. pl.*) string beans
*****haut(e)** high; loud (*voice*);
  au haut (de) in/at the top
  (of); **en haut** upstairs
herbe (*f.*) grass
heure (*f.*) hour; **à l'heure** on
  time; **à tout à l'heure** see
  you later; **de bonne heure**
  early
heureux (-euse) happy
hier yesterday
histoire (*f.*) story, history
hiver (*m.*) winter
homme (*m.*) man
honnête honest
honneur (*m.*) honor; **tableau
  d'honneur** honor roll
*****honte** (*f.*) shame; **avoir honte**
  to be ashamed
hôpital (*m.*) hospital
horaire (*f.*) schedule

horloge (*f.*) clock
*****hors** outside
*****hors-d'œuvre** (*m.*) appetizer
hôtel (*m.*) hotel
*****huit** eight
hypermarché (*m.*) large
  supermarket

ici here
idée (*f.*) idea
il he, it
il y a there is/are; **il n'y a pas
  de quoi** you're welcome
île (*f.*) island
ils they
image (*f.*) picture
imaginer to imagine
immeuble (*m.*) apartment
  building
imperméable (*m.*) raincoat
indiquer to indicate
indulgent(e) indulgent, lenient
infirmier (-ière) nurse
informations (*f. pl.*) news
informatique (*f.*) computer
  science
ingénieur (*m.*) engineer
injuste unfair
insecte (*m.*) insect
instituteur (-trice) teacher
instruction (*f.*) instruction,
  direction
intensité (*f.*) intensity
interdit(e) forbidden,
  prohibited
intéressant(e) interesting
intéresser to interest
intuitif (-ive) intuitive
inutile useless
invité(e) guest
inviter to invite
itinéraire (*m.*) itinerary

jaloux (-ouse) jealous
jamais never, ever; **jamais de
  la vie** out of the question;
  ne... jamais never

jambe (*f.*) leg
jambon (*m.*) ham
janvier (*m.*) January
jardin (*m.*) garden
jaune yellow; **jaune** (*m.*) yolk (*of egg*)
je I
jeter to throw; **se jeter** to empty (*river*)
jeu (*m.*) game; **jeu de cartes** card game
jeudi (*m.*) Thursday
jeune young
joie (*f.*) joy
joli(e) pretty
jouer to play; **jouer à** to play (*a game/a sport*); **jouer de** to play (*a musical instrument*); **se jouer** to be played
jour (*m.*) day; **jour de congé** day off; **jour férié** legal holiday
journal (*m.*) (*pl.* **-aux**) newspaper; journal
journée (*f.*) day
joyeux (-euse) joyous
juge (*m.*) judge
juillet (*m.*) July
juin (*m.*) June
jumeau (*m.*) (*pl.* **-aux**) twin
jupe (*f.*) skirt
jus (*m.*) juice
jusqu'à until
juste fair; right

la the; her, it
là there
lac (*m.*) lake
laid(e) ugly
laisser to leave
lait (*m.*) milk
laitue (*f.*) lettuce
lampe (*f.*) lamp
lancer to throw
langue (*f.*) language
lapin (*m.*) rabbit
latin (*m.*) Latin

laver to wash; **laver la vaisselle** to do the dishes; **machine à laver** washing machine; **se laver** to wash oneself
le the; him, it
leçon (*f.*) lesson
lecture (*f.*) reading
léger (-ère) light (weight)
légume (*m.*) vegetable
lentement slowly
les the; them, to them
lettre (*f.*) letter; **boîte aux lettres** (*f.*) mailbox; **en toutes lettres** in full
leur their; to them
lever to raise, lift; **se lever** to get up
librairie (*f.*) bookstore
libre free
lieu (*m.*) place; **au lieu (de)** instead (of)
ligne (*f.*) line
limonade (*f.*) lemon soda
lion (*m.*) lion
liquide (*m.*) liquid
lire (*p.p.* **lu**) to read
liste (*f.*) list
lit (*m.*) bed; **faire le lit** to make the bed
living (*m.*) living room
livre (*m.*) book
livret (*m.*) booklet
loin (de) far (from)
long(ue) long; **de long en large** back and forth
longtemps a long time
loterie (*f.*) lottery
louer to rent
loup (*m.*) wolf
lourd(e) heavy
lui he, him, to him, her, to her
lundi (*m.*) Monday
lune (*f.*) moon
lunettes (*f. pl.*) eyeglasses; **lunettes de soleil** sunglasses
luxueux (-euse) luxurious
lycée (*m.*) high school

ma my
machine (*f.*) machine; **machine à écrire** typewriter; **machine à laver** washing machine
madame (*f.*) (*pl.* **mesdames**) Madam, Mrs.
mademoiselle (*f.*) (*pl.* **mesdemoiselles**) Miss
magasin (*m.*) store; **grand magasin** department store
magnétoscope (*m.*) VCR
magnifique magnificent
mai (*m.*) May
maigre thin
maigrir to become thin
maillot (*m.*) jersey; **maillot de bain** bathing suit
main (*f.*) hand
maintenant now
mais but
maison (*f.*) house; **maison des jeunes et de la culture** (M.J.C.) youth center
mal bad(ly); **aller mal** to feel poorly; **avoir mal à** to have an ache in; **mal de dents** (*m.*) toothache
malade sick
maladie (*f.*) illness, sickness
malgré in spite of
malheureux (-euse) unhappy
maman (*f.*) mom
manger to eat
manteau (*m.*) coat
maquiller to apply make-up; **se maquiller** to put on one's make-up
marché (*m.*) market; **bon marché** inexpensive
marcher to walk; to work, to function
mardi (*m.*) Tuesday
mari (*m.*) husband
marier to marry; **se marier (avec)** to marry
marron brown

mars (*m.*) March
match (*m.*) match, game
matériel scolaire (*m.*) school supplies
mathématiques (*f. pl.*) mathematics
maths (*f. pl.*) math
matière (*f.*) subject
matin (*m.*) morning
matinée (*f.*) morning
mauvais(e) bad; **faire mauvais** to be bad (*weather*)
mauve purple
me me, to me
mécanicien(ne) mechanic
méchant(e) naughty, wicked
médecin (*m.*) doctor
médicament (*m.*) medicine
meilleur(e) best
mélanger to mix
même same (*adj.*); even (*adv.*)
menacer to threaten
ménage (*m.*) household; **faire le ménage** to do the housework
mener to lead
mensonge (*m.*) lie
mentionner to mention
mer (*f.*) sea; **au bord de la mer** to/on the seashore
merci thank you
mercredi (*m.*) Wednesday
mère (*f.*) mother
merveilleux (-euse) marvelous
mes my
météo (*f.*) weather report
métro (*m.*) subway
mettre (*p.p.* **mis**) to put (on); **mettre la table** to set the table; **mettre le couvert** to set the table; **se mettre à** to begin to; **se mettre en route** to start out
meuble (*m.*) piece of furniture; **meubles** (*m. pl.*) furniture
midi (*m.*) noon; south

mieux better; **aimer mieux** to prefer; **faire de son mieux** to do one's best
milieu (*m.*) center, middle; **au milieu** in the middle
mille (**mil** *in dates*) (one) thousand
milliard (*m.*) billion
million (*m.*) million
mince skinny
minéral(e) mineral; **eau minérale** mineral water
minuit (*m.*) midnight
minute (*f.*) minute
miroir (*m.*) mirror
mobylette (*f.*) moped
moderne modern
moi I, me
moins less, minus; **au moins** at least; **moins (de)** less, fewer
mois (*m.*) month
moment (*m.*) moment
mon my
monde (*m.*) world; **tout le monde** everybody; **faire le tour du monde** to go around the world
monsieur (*m.*) (*pl.* **messieurs**) sir, gentleman, Mr.
montagne (*f.*) mountain
monter to go up, to climb; to carry up; **monter à bicyclette** to go bicycle riding
montre (*f.*) watch
montrer to show
morceau (*m.*) piece
mort(e) dead
mot (*m.*) word
mouchoir (*m.*) handkerchief
mourir (*p.p.* **mort**) to die
mousquetaire (*m.*) musketeer
mousse (*f.*) mousse; **mousse au chocolat** chocolate mousse
mouton (*m.*) sheep

moyen (*m.*) means; **moyen de transport** means of transportation
mur (*m.*) wall
musée (*m.*) museum

n'est-ce pas? isn't that so?
nager to swim
naïf (-ve) naive
naissance (*f.*) birth
naître (*p.p.* **né**) to be born
natation (*f.*) swimming
ne... jamais never; **ne... pas** not; **ne... personne** nobody, no one; **ne... plus** no longer, no more, anymore; **ne... rien** nothing
nécessaire necessary
négliger to neglect
neiger to snow
nerveux (-euse) nervous
nettoyage (*m.*) cleaning
nettoyer to clean
neuf (-ve) new
neuf nine
neveu (*m.*) nephew
nez (*m.*) nose
nièce (*f.*) niece
Noël (*m.*) Christmas
noir(e) black; **noir** (*m.*) darkness
nom (*m.*) name
non no
nord (*m.*) north
nos our
note (*f.*) note, grade
noter to note
notre our
nous we, us, to us
nouveau, nouvel (*f.* **nouvelle**) new; **de nouveau** again
nouvelles (*f. pl.*) news
novembre (*m.*) November
nuage (*m.*) cloud
nuit (*f.*) night; **table de nuit** (*f.*) night table

numéro (*m.*) number; **numéro de téléphone** telephone number

obéir (**à**) to obey
occasion (*f.*) occasion, opportunity
occupé(e) busy
octobre (*m.*) October
œil (*m.*) (*pl.* **yeux**) eye; **un coup d'œil** glance
œuf (*m.*) egg
œuvre (*f.*) work
offrir (*p.p.* **offert**) to offer
oignon (*m.*) onion
oiseau (*m.*) bird
on one, we, you, they, people (*in general*)
oncle (*m.*) uncle
ongle (*m.*) nail
onze eleven
ordinaire ordinary
ordinateur (*m.*) computer
ordonner to order
ordures (*f. pl.*) garbage
oreille (*f.*) ear
orteil (*m.*) toe
orthographe (*f.*) spelling
ôter to remove, take off
ou or
où where
oublier to forget
ouest (*m.*) west
oui yes
ours (*m.*) bear
ouvrier (**-ière**) factory worker
ouvrir (*p.p.* **ouvert**) to open

page (*f.*) page
pain (*m.*) bread; **pain grillé** toast
paire (*f.*) pair
paix (*f.*) peace
palais (*m.*) palace
pantalon (*m.*) pants
papier (*m.*) paper

paquet (*m.*) package
par by, through, per; **par conséquent** consequently; **par exemple** for example; **par jour** per day; **par rapport à** with regard to; **par terre** on the ground
parapluie (*m.*) umbrella
parc (*m.*) park; parking; **parc d'attractions** amusement park
parce que because
pardessus (*m.*) overcoat
pardonner to forgive, to excuse
paresseux (**-euse**) lazy
parfait(e) perfect
parfois sometimes
parfum (*m.*) perfume
parler to speak
partager to share, to divide
partie (*f.*) part; **faire partie de** to belong to
partir to leave, go away; **à partir de** from
partout everywhere
pas not; **pas du tout** not at all; **pas encore** not yet; **ne... pas** not
passé(e) past; **l'année passée** last year
passer to pass; to spend (*time*); **passer l'aspirateur** to vacuum; **passer un examen** to take a test; **se passer** to happen
patin (*m.*) skate; **patin à glace** ice skate, ice skating; **faire du patin à glace** to go ice skating
patiner to skate
pâtissier (**-ière**) pastry maker
patron(ne) boss; patron saint
pauvre poor
payer to pay (for)
pays (*m.*) country
paysan(ne) peasant

peau (*f.*) skin
pêche (*f.*) peach
pêche (*f.*) fishing; **aller à la pêche** to go fishing
pêcher to fish
peigne (*m.*) comb
peigner to comb; **se peigner** to comb one's hair
peindre (*p.p.* **peint**) to paint
peintre (*m.*) painter
pelouse (*f.*) lawn
pendant during; **pendant que** while
penderie (*f.*) closet
pendule (*f.*) clock
penser to think; to intend
perdre to lose; **perdre son temps** to waste one's time
père (*m.*) father
permettre (*p.p.* **permis**) to allow, permit
permis (*m.*) permit; **permis de conduire** driver's license
personne (*f.*) person
personne (**ne**) nobody, no one; **ne... personne** nobody, no one
peser to weigh
petit(e) little, small; **petit ami** (*m.*) boyfriend; **petite amie** (*f.*) girlfriend; **petit-fils** (*m.*) grandson; **petit déjeuner** (*m.*) breakfast; **petits pois** (*m. pl.*) peas
peu (**de**) little, few; **à peu près** about, approximately; **un peu** a little
peuple (*m.*) people (of a nation)
peur (*f.*) fear; **avoir peur de** to be afraid of
peut-être perhaps, maybe
photo (*f.*) photo, picture; **prendre une photo** to take a picture
phrase (*f.*) phrase, sentence
physique (*f.*) physics

pièce (*f.*) play
pied (*m.*) foot; **aller à pied** to walk, go on foot
piscine (*f.*) swimming pool
placard (*m.*) cabinet, cupboard
place (*f.*) seat, place, square; **en place** in place
placer to place, set
plage (*f.*) beach
plaisir (*m.*) pleasure; **faire plaisir (à)** to please
plat (*m.*) dish
plein(e) full; **en plein air** outdoors
pleurer to cry
pleuvoir (*p.p.* **plu**) to rain
plonger, to plunge, dive
pluie (*f.*) rain
plus (de) more; **plus tard** later; **ne... plus** no longer, no more, anymore
plusieurs several
pneu (*m.*) tire
poche (*f.*) pocket
poème (*m.*) poem
poésie (*f.*) poetry
poire (*f.*) pear
poisson (*m.*) fish
poitrine (*f.*) chest
poivre (*m.*) pepper
poli(e) polite
policier (-ière) police
pomme (*f.*) apple
pomme de terre (*f.*) potato
pont (*m.*) bridge
port (*m.*) port
porte (*f.*) door, gate
portable (*m.*) cell phone
portefeuille (*m.*) wallet
porter to carry; to wear
poser to place; to ask (*questions*)
posséder to possess, to own
poste (*f.*) post office; **bureau de poste** (*m.*) post office
potage (*m.*) soup
poule (*f.*) chicken
poulet (*m.*) chicken

poupée (*f.*) doll
pour for, in order to
pourquoi why
pousser to push; to grow; **pousser un soupir de soulagement** to breathe a sigh of relief
pouvoir (*p.p.* **pu**) to be able to, can
pratique practical
pratiquer to practice
précieux (-euse) precious, important
préférer to prefer
premier (-ière) first; **premier ministre** (*m.*) prime minister
prendre to take (*p.p.* **pris**); **prendre soin** to take care
préparatifs (*m.pl.*) preparations
préparer to prepare; **se préparer** to prepare oneself
près (de) near; **à peu près** about, approximately
présenter to introduce; to offer
pressé(e) in a hurry
prêt(e) ready
prétendre to claim
prêter to lend
printemps (*m.*) spring
privé(e) private
prix (*m.*) prize; price
problème (*m.*) problem
prochain(e) next
proche nearby
produit (*m.*) product
professeur (*m.*) (*coll.* **prof**) teacher
profiterole (*f.*) cream puff with chocolate sauce
programme (*m.*) program
programmeur (-euse) programmer
progrès (*m.*) progress
projet (*m.*) project
promenade (*f.*) walk; **faire une promenade** to go for a walk
promener to walk;

se promener to take a walk
prononcer to pronounce; to declare
propriétaire (*m.*) owner
protéger to protect
prune (*f.*) plum
public (*m.*) public, audience
publier to publish
puis then
puisque since
pull (*m.*) pullover, sweater
punir to punish
pupitre (*m.*) pupil's desk

quand when
quarante forty
quart (*m.*) quarter
quartier (*m.*) neighborhood
quatorze fourteen
quatre four
quatre-vingt-dix ninety
quatre-vingts eighty
quatrième fourth
que that, whom, which; what; than; **ce que** that which, what; **qu'est-ce que** what
quel(le) what, which; what a
quelque some; **quelques** (*m./f. pl.*) a few, some
quelqu'un someone
quelque chose something
quelquefois sometimes
question (*f.*) question
qui who, whom, which, that
quinze fifteen
quitter to leave
quoi what; **(il n'y a) pas de quoi** you're welcome

raconter to tell; to describe
radio (*f.*) radio
rafraîchissement (*m.*) refreshment
ragoût (*m.*) stew
raisin (*m.*) grape
raison (*f.*) reason; **avoir raison** to be right

ramasser to pick up
ramener to bring back
rang (*m.*) row
ranger to put away; to put in order; to straighten, to arrange, to tidy
rappeler to recall; **se rappeler** to remember
raquette (*f.*) racket
raser to shave; **se raser** to shave (oneself)
recette (*f.*) recipe
recevoir (*p.p.* **reçu**) to receive
recherche (*f.*) search
recommander to recommend
récompense (*f.*) reward
refaire to redo
refermer to close again
réfléchir to reflect, to think
refuser (**de**) to refuse (to)
regarder to look at, to watch
régime (*m.*) diet
règle (*f.*) ruler
règlement (*m.*) rules
régler to set
regretter (**de**) to regret (to)
regulièrement regularly
remercier to thank
remettre (*p.p.* **remis**) to put back; to deliver
remplacer to replace
remplir to fill
rencontrer to meet
rendre to give back, to return; **rendre visite** (**à**) to visit
renoncer (**à**) to give up, renounce
renseignements (*m. pl.*) information
rentrée (*f.*) return; **rentrée scolaire** return to school
rentrer to return
renvoyer to send back; to fire
réparer to repair
repas (*m.*) meal
répéter to repeat
répondre (**à**) to answer

réponse (*f.*) answer
reposer to rest; **se reposer** to rest, to relax
résoudre (*p.p.* **résolu**) to solve, to resolve
ressembler (**à**) to resemble; **se ressembler** to look alike
rester to remain, to stay
résultat (*m.*) result
retard (*m.*) lateness; **en retard** late
retourner to return
réussir (**à**) to succeed (in)
réveil (*m.*) alarm clock
réveiller to awaken; **se réveiller** to wake up
revenir (*p.p.* **revenu**) to come back
rêver (**de**) to dream (of)
revoir (*p.p.* **revu**) to see again; **au revoir** goodbye
revue (*f.*) magazine
rez-de-chaussée (*m.*) ground floor
rhume (*m.*) cold
rien (**ne**) nothing; **de rien** you're welcome; **ne... rien** nothing
rire to laugh
rivière (*f.*) stream
robe (*f.*) dress
roman (*m.*) novel
rompre to break
rose pink
rôtir to roast
rouge (*m.*) red; **rouge à lèvres** lipstick
rougir to blush
rouler to roll along
route (*f.*) road, route; **en route** on the way; **se mettre en route** to start out
roux (*f.* **rousse**) red (hair)
rue (*f.*) street

sa his, her
sable (*m.*) sand

sac (*m.*) bag, sack, pocketbook; **sac à dos** backpack
saisir to seize, to grab
saison (*f.*) season
saladier (*m.*) salad bowl
sale dirty
salle (*f.*) room; **salle à manger** dining room; **salle de bains** bathroom; **salle de classe** classroom; **salle de séjour** living room
salon (*m.*) living room; lounge
salut hi
samedi (*m.*) Saturday
sans without; **sans doute** without a doubt
santé (*f.*) health
sauver to save
savoir (*p.p.* **su**) to know (how to)
scolaire school; **matériel** (*m.*) **scolaire** school supplies; **rentrée** (*f.*) **scolaire** return to school
se (to) himself, (to) herself, (to) oneself, (to) themselves
secrétaire (*m./f.*) secretary
secrètement secretly
seize sixteen
séjour (*m.*) stay; family room; **salle de séjour** (*f.*) family room
sel (*m.*) salt
selon according to
semaine (*f.*) week
sept seven
septembre (*m.*) September
série (*f.*) series
sérieux (**-euse**) serious
serveur (**-euse**) waiter, waitress
serviette (*f.*) briefcase; napkin
servir (**de**) to serve (as)
ses his, her
seul(e) only, single, alone
seulement only
si if; yes; so

s'il te plaît please
s'il vous plaît please
situé(e) situated
six six
sixième sixth
ski (*m.*) ski; **ski nautique** water skiing; **faire du ski** to go skiing
société (*f.*) company; society
sœur (*f.*) sister
soie (*f.*) silk
soif (*f.*) thirst; **avoir soif** to be thirsty
soin (*m.*) care; **prendre soin (de)** to take care (of)
soir (*m.*) evening
soirée (*f.*) evening
soixante sixty
soixante-dix seventy
solaire sun
soleil (*m.*) sun; **coucher de soleil** (*m.*) sunset; **lunettes de soleil** (*f.*) sunglasses; **faire du soleil** to be sunny
somme (*f.*) sum
sommeil (*m.*) sleep; **avoir sommeil** to be sleepy
son his, her, its
son (*m.*) sound
songer (**à**) to think (of)
sonner to ring
sorte (*f.*) sort, type
sortir to go out
souhaiter to wish
soulagement (*m.*) relief
soulier (*m.*) shoe
soupir (*m.*) sigh; **pousser un soupir de soulagement** to breathe a sigh of relief
sous under
sous-sol (*m.*) basement
souvent often
spectacle (*m.*) show
sport (*m.*) sport; **voiture de sport** sports car; **faire du sport** to play sports
sportif (-ve) sporty, athletic

stade (*m.*) stadium
station-service (*f.*) service station
store (*m.*) shade, blind
studieux (-euse) studious
stylo (*m.*) pen
succès (*m.*) success
sucre (*m.*) sugar
sud (*m.*) south
suggérer to suggest
suisse Swiss
suivre (*p.p.* **suivi**) to follow
supermarché (*m.*) supermarket
sur on, upon
sûr(e) sure; **bien sûr** of course
surtout especially
sympathique likable, nice

ta your
table (*f.*) table; **table de nuit** night table; **mettre la table** to set the table
tableau (*m.*) chalkboard; painting; **tableau d'honneur** honor roll
tant so much/many; **tant pis** too bad
tante (*f.*) aunt
tapis (*m.*) rug
tard late; **plus tard** later
tarif (*m.*) rate
tarte (*f.*) pie
tasse (*f.*) cup
te you, to you
tel(le) such
téléphone (*m.*) telephone; **(téléphone) portable** cell phone; **au téléphone** on the telephone; **coup de téléphone** telephone call; **numéro de téléphone** telephone number
tellement so
temps (*m.*) time; weather; **emploi du temps** schedule, program; **de temps en temps** from time to time; **perdre son**

temps to waste one's time; **tout le temps** all the time
tennis (*m.*) tennis
tennis (*f.*) tennis sneaker
tente (*f.*) tent
terminer to end
terrasse (*f.*) terrace
terre (*f.*) earth, land; **par terre** on the ground
terrible terrible
tête (*f.*) head
théâtre (*m.*) theater
thé (*m.*) tea
thon (*m.*) tunafish
tigre (*m.*) tiger
timbre (*m.*) stamp
toi you
toilettes (*f. pl.*) toilet
tomber to fall; **tomber amoureux** to fall in love
ton your
tondre to mow
tort (*m.*) error; **avoir tort** to be wrong
tôt early, soon
toucher to touch; **toucher un chèque** to cash a check
toujours always, still
tour (*m.*) tour; **faire le tour du monde** to go around the world
tour (*f.*) tower
tourner to turn
tout everything, quite, entirely
tout(e) (*m. pl.* **tous**) all; every; **à tout à l'heure** see you later; **après tout** after all; **tous les jours** every day; **tout à coup** suddenly; **tout à fait** entirely; **tout d'un coup** suddenly; **tout de suite** immediately; **tout droit** straight ahead; **tout le monde** everybody; **tout le temps** all the time
toux (*f.*) cough
trahir to betray

train (*m.*) train; **être en train de** to be in the process of (do)ing
traiter to treat
tramway (*m.*) streetcar
tranquille tranquil, calm
transport (*m.*) transportation; **moyen de transport** (*m.*) means of transportation
travail (*m.*) (*pl.* **-aux**) work; **travaux ménagers** housework
travailler to work
travers: à travers across, through
traverser to cross
treize thirteen
trente thirty
très very
triste sad
trois three
trop (**de**) too; too many, too much
trottoir (*m.*) sidewalk
trousse (*f.*) pencil case
trouver to find; **se trouver** to be (found)
tu you (*fam.*)

un(e) a, an, one
usé(e) worn
utile useful
utiliser to use

vacances (*f. pl.*) vacation;

colonie de vacances (*f.*) camp
vache (*f.*) cow
vaisselle (*f.*) dishes; **faire, laver la vaisselle** to do the dishes
vanille (*f.*) vanilla
veau (*m.*) veal
vélo (*m.*) bicycle
vendeur (-euse) salesperson
vendre to sell
vendredi (*m.*) Friday
venir (*p.p.* **venu**) to come
vent (*m.*) wind; **faire du vent** to be windy
ventre (*m.*) stomach
verité (*f.*) truth
verre (*m.*) glass
vers towards
vert(e) green; **haricots verts** (*m. pl.*) string beans; **plante verte** potted plant
veste (*f.*) jacket
vêtements (*m.pl.*) clothes; **vêtements sport** sport clothes
vêtu(e) dressed
viande (*f.*) meat
vide empty
vie (*f.*) life
vieux, vieil (*f.* **vieille**) old
vif (**vive**) lively
ville (*f.*) city; **en ville** downtown
vin (*m.*) wine

vingt twenty
visage (*m.*) face
vite rapidly, quickly
vivre (*p.p.* **vécu**) to live
voici here!, here is/are
voie (*f.*) track
voilà there!, there is/are
voir (*p.p.* **vu**) to see
voisin(e) neighbor
voiture (*f.*) car; **voiture de sport** sports car; **aller en voiture** to go by car
voix (*f.*) voice; **à haute voix/à voix haute** out loud; **à voix basse** in a low voice
vol (*m.*) flight
voler to fly
voleur (*m.*) robber
vos your
votre your
vouloir (*p.p.* **voulu**) to want
vous you, to you
voyage (*m.*) trip, voyage; **chèque de voyage** traveler's check; **faire un voyage** to take a trip
voyager to travel
vrai(e) true
vraiment truly, really

y to it/them, in it/them, on it/them; there; **il y a** there is
yeux (*m. pl*) eyes

English-French Vocabulary

The English-French vocabulary is sufficient for the needs of this book.

ABBREVIATIONS

(*adj.*)	adjective	(*inf.*)	infinitive
(*adv.*)	adverb	(*m.*)	masculine
(*f.*)	feminine	(*pl.*)	plural

A.M. du matin

able: to be able pouvoir

active actif (-ive)

actress actrice (*f.*)

add ajouter

address adresse (*f.*)

advance avance (*f.*);
 in advance à l'avance

afraid: be afraid avoir peur

after après

afternoon après-midi (*m.*)

again encore une fois

age âge (*m.*)

airplane avion (*m.*)

all tout(e) (*m. pl.* tous); **all the
 time** tout le temps

almost presque

alone seul(e)

also aussi

always toujours

and et

another un autre (*m.*)

answer répondre (à);
 réponse (*f.*)

anymore ne... plus

apple pomme (*f.*) ; **apple pie**
 tarte aux pommes (*f.*)

arm bras (*m.*)

around autour (de)

ask (for) demander

at à; **at home** à la maison

aunt tante (*f.*)

autumn automne (*m.*)

back dos (*m.*)

backpack sac à dos (*m.*)

bad mauvais(e)

bag sac (*m.*)

baker boulanger (-ère);
 pâtissier (*f.* -ière)

bank banque (*f.*); (*river*) rive (*f.*)

basement sous-sol (*m.*)

bathing suit maillot de bain
 (*m.*)

bathroom salle de bains (*f.*)

be être; **to be ... years old**
 avoir... ans

beach plage (*f.*)

beautiful beau, bel (*f.* belle)

because car, parce que

become devenir; **become fat**
 grossir

bed lit (*m.*); **go to bed** se
 coucher

bedroom chambre (*f.*)

before avant (de)

beginning commencement (*m.*)

behind derrière

bell cloche (*f.*)

between entre

bicycle bicyclette (*f.*), vélo (*m.*)

big grand(e)

black noir(e)

blue bleu(e)

blush rougir

boat bateau (*m.*)

book livre (*m.*)

bookstore librairie (*f.*)

boot botte (*f.*)

bore ennuyer;

 to get bored s'ennuyer

borrow emprunter

bother ennuyer, gêner

bottle bouteille (*f.*)

box boîte (*f.*)

boy garçon (*m.*)

bread pain (*m.*)

breakfast petit déjeuner (*m.*)

bring apporter

brother frère (*m.*)

brush brosser; **brush
 (oneself)** se brosser

build bâtir

but mais

butcher boucher (-ère);
 butcher shop boucherie (*f.*)

butter beurre (*m.*)

buy acheter

by par ; **by bus** en bus

cake gâteau (*m.*)

call appeler; téléphoner (à)

can pouvoir

candy bonbon (*m.*)

car voiture (*f.*)

card carte (*f.*); **postcard** carte
 postale (*f.*)

castle château (*m.*)

cat chat (*m.*)

cathedral cathédrale (*f.*)

celebration fête (*f.*)

chair chaise (*f.*)

chalk craie (*f.*)

change changer; **change one's
 mind** changer d'avis

charming charmant(e)
chat bavarder
cheap bon marché
cheese fromage *(m.)*
chicken poulet *(m.)*
child enfant *(m. / f.)*
chocolate chocolat *(m.)*;
  chocolate mousse mousse
  au chocolat *(f.)*; **chocolate
  cake** gâteau au chocolat *(m.)*
choose choisir
church église *(f.)*
city ville *(f.)*
clean nettoyer
clock horloge *(f.)*
close fermer
closet penderie *(f.)*
clothes vêtements *(m. pl.)*
coat manteau *(m.)*
cold froid; **to be cold** *(person)*
  avoir froid; **to be cold**
  (weather) faire froid
come venir
comfortable confortable
compact disc disque compact
  (m.); compact *(m.)*; CD
concert concert *(m.)*; **rock
  concert** concert de rock
cook cuire; cuisiner, faire la
  cuisine; *(m/f)* cuisinier (-ière)
cookie biscuit *(m.)*
country campagne *(f.)*; pays
  (m.)
courageous courageux (-euse)
course cours *(m.)* **of course**
  bien sûr
cow vache *(f.)*
criticize critiquer
cross croix *(f.)*
cry pleurer
cup tasse *(f.)*
cure guérir

dance danser
daughter fille *(f.)*
day jour *(m.)*; journée *(f.)*

decide décider (de)
defend défendre
delicious délicieux (-ieuse)
department département *(m.)*
desk bureau *(m.)*, **pupil's desk**
  pupitre *(m.)*
dictionary dictionnaire *(m.)*
die mourir
difficult difficile
dining room salle à manger *(f.)*
dinner *(m.)*; dîner; **to eat
  dinner** dîner
disobey désobéir
dive plonger
do faire
doctor docteur *(m.)*, médecin
  (m.)
dog chien *(m.)*
door porte *(f.)*
down: go down descendre
downtown en ville
dozen douzaine *(f.)*
dress habiller; **dress (oneself)**
  s'habiller
dress robe *(f.)*
during pendant

each chaque
ear oreille *(f.)*
easy facile
eat manger; **eat dinner** dîner
egg œuf *(m.)*
empty vider
end fin *(f.)*
ending fin *(f.)*
English anglais *(m.)*
enter entrer
entire entier (-ière)
entrance entrée *(f.)*
eraser gomme *(f.)*; éponge à
  effacer *(f.)*
evening soir *(m.)*
every chaque; tout (tous,
  toute, toutes); **every day**
  tous les jours
everybody tout le monde *(m.)*

everyone tout le monde *(m.)*
everything tout *(m.)*
exchange échanger; **exchange
  letters** correspondre
expensive cher *(f. chère)*
explain expliquer
eye œil *(m.)* *(pl yeux)*

face figure *(f.)*, visage *(m.)*
false faux *(f. fausse)*
family famille *(f.)*
famous célèbre
far loin (de)
farmer fermier *(f. fermière)*
fast vite, rapidement
fat gros(se); **become fat**
  grossir
favorite favori(te), préféré(e)
fear peur *(f.)*; **to be afraid**
  avoir peur
fill remplir
find trouver
finger doigt *(m.)*
finish finir, achever, terminer
fish pêcher, aller à la pêche
fish poisson *(m.)*
flight vol *(m.)*
flower fleur *(f.)*
food nourriture *(f.)*, aliments
  (m. pl.)
foot pied *(m.)*
football football américain *(m.)*
for pour
forget oublier
frank franc(he)
French français
friend ami *(m.)*, copain *(m.)* *(f.
  copine)*, camarade *(m. / f.)*
friendly amical(e), aimable
from de; **from the** du, de la,
  de l', des
front: in front of devant
fruit fruit *(m.)*; **fruit store**
  fruiterie *(f.)*
full plein
fun: have fun s'amuser

funny drôle, comique, amusant

game match (*m.*)

garage garage (*m.*)

garbage ordures (*f. pl.*)

garden jardin (*m.*)

gasoline essence (*f.*); **gas station** station-service (*f.*)

generous généreux (-euse)

gently doucement

get up se lever; **get dressed** s'habiller

gift cadeau (*m.*)

girl fille (*f.*)

girlfriend petite amie (*f.*)

give donner

glass verre (*m.*)

glasses lunettes (*f. pl.*)

go aller; **go back home** rentrer; **go down** descendre; **go out** sortir

good bon(ne); **have a good time** s'amuser

good-bye au revoir

grandfather grand-père (*m.*)

grandmother grand-mère (*f.*)

grandparents (*m. pl.*) grands-parents

great formidable, super

grow grandir

guard garder

hair cheveux (*m. pl.*)

ham jambon (*m.*)

hand main (*f.*)

handsome beau, bel (*f.* belle

happy content, heureux (-euse)

hat chapeau (*m.*)

head tête (*f.*)

hear entendre

heavy lourd(e)

help aider

here ici; **here is, here are** voici

high haut

history histoire (*f.*)

home maison (*f.*); **(at) home** à la maison; **at (the home**

of) chez

homework devoirs (*m. pl.*); **do homework** faire les devoirs

honest honnête

hope espérer

horse cheval (*m.*) (*pl.* chevaux)

hot chaud(e); to be hot (*person*) avoir chaud; **to be hot** (*weather*) faire chaud

hour heure (*f.*)

house maison (*f.*)

how comment; **how much, many** combien (de)

huge énorme

hurry (up) se dépêcher

ice cream glace (*f.*)

ice skating patin à glace (*m.*); **go ice skating** faire du patin à glace

idea idée (*f.*)

if si

immediately immédiatement, tout de suite

in dans, en, à

inexpensive bon marché

instead (of) au lieu (de)

intend compter

interesting intéressant(e)

island île (*f.*)

jacket veste (*f.*)

job emploi (*m.*)

keep garder

key clef (*f.*)

kind gentil(le), aimable

king roi (*m.*)

kitchen cuisine (*f.*)

knife couteau (*m.*)

know connaître, savoir

lake lac (*m.*)

lamp lampe (*f.*)

large grand(e)

last dernier (-ière); **last night**

hier soir

late tard

later plus tard

lawn pelouse (*f.*)

lawyer avocat (*m.*)

lazy paresseux (-euse)

lead mener

least: at least au moins

leave partir

left gauche

lemonade citronnade (*f.*)

lend prêter

lesson leçon (*f.*)

letter lettre (*f.*)

library bibliothèque (*f.*)

life vie (*f.*)

light léger (*f.* légère)

like aimer

listen (to) écouter

little petit(e); peu

live habiter, demeurer, vivre

living room salon (*m.*)

long long(ue); **a long time** longtemps

longer: no longer ne...plus

look regarder

loose-leaf classeur (*m.*)

lose perdre

lot: a lot beaucoup; **lots of** beaucoup de

loud fort(e)

love aimer; amour (*m.*)

loyal fidèle

lunch déjeuner (*m.*)

magazine magazine (*m.*), revue (*f.*)

magnificent magnifique

make faire

make-up maquillage (*m.*); **to put make-up** se maquiller

mall centre commercial (*m.*)

man homme (*m.*)

many beaucoup (de); **how many** combien (de)

map carte (*f.*)

marry épouser, se marier avec

matter: it doesn't matter ça ne fait rien

meal repas *(m.)*

meat viande *(f.)*

mechanic mécanicien(ne)

meet rencontrer, faire la connaissance de

middle milieu *(m.)*, centre *(m.)*

midnight minuit *(m.)*

mind esprit *(m.)*; **change one's mind** changer d'avis

mistake faute *(f.)*, erreur *(f.)*

modern moderne

money argent *(m.)*

month mois *(m.)*

more plus

morning matin *(m.)*

mother mère *(f.)*

mountain montagne *(f.)*

move déménager

movie film *(m.)*; **movies** cinéma *(m.)*

much beaucoup; **how much** combien (de)

museum musée *(m.)*

name nom *(m.)*

near près (de)

neck cou *(m.)*

need besoin *(m.)*; **need** avoir besoin de

neighborhood quartier *(m.)*

nephew *(m.)* neveu

never ne... jamais, jamais

new nouveau, nouvel *(f. nouvelle)*

newspaper journal *(m.)*

next prochain(e)

nice sympathique, agréable, gentil(le); **to be nice** *(weather)* faire beau

niece nièce *(f.)*

night nuit *(f.)*, soir *(m.)*; **night table** table de nuit *(f.)*

no non

nobody personne (ne)

noon midi *(m.)*

nose nez *(m.)*

not ne... pas

notebook cahier *(m.)*

nothing rien (ne)

now maintenant

number numéro *(m.)*; **telephone number** numéro de téléphone

nut noix *(f.)*

obey obéir

of de; **of course** bien sûr

office bureau *(m.)*

often souvent

old vieux, vieil *(f. vieille)*; **to be . . . years old** avoir... ans

on sur, de; **on time** à l'heure

once une fois

one un(e); **no one** personne

only seul *(adj.)*; seulement *(adv.)*

open ouvrir; **open up** s'ouvrir

opportunity occasion *(f.)*

organize organiser

out: go out sortir

over there là-bas

overcoat *(m.)* manteau

P.M. de l'après-midi, du soir

package paquet *(m.)*

painting tableau *(m.)*

pair paire *(f.)*

palace palais *(m.)*

pants pantalon *(m.)*

paper papier *(m.)*

park parc *(m.)*

party fête *(f.)*, boum *(f.)*

passport passeport *(m.)*

pastry pâtisserie *(f.)*; **pastry shop** pâtisserie *(f.)*

pay (for) payer; **pay attention** faire attention

peace paix *(f.)*

pen stylo *(m.)*

pen pal correspondant(e)

pencil crayon *(m.)*; **pencil case** trousse *(f.)*

people *(m. pl.)* gens

phone téléphone *(m.)*; **phone book** annuaire *(m.)*; **phone booth** cabine *(f.)*; **phone number** numéro de téléphone *(m.)*

picture image *(f.)*, illustration *(f.)*, photo *(f.)*

pie tarte *(f.)*

plane avion *(m.)*

play jouer; **play** *(an instrument)* jouer de; **play** *(a sport)* jouer à, faire du

please s'il te plaît, s'il vous plaît

pleased content(e), heureux (-euse)

pleasure plaisir *(m.)*

plus et; plus

pool piscine *(f.)*

poor pauvre

post office poste *(f.)*, bureau de poste *(m.)*

postcard carte postale *(f.)*

poster poster *(m.)*, affiche *(f.)*

potato pomme de terre *(f.)*

prefer préférer, aimer mieux

prepare préparer

present cadeau *(m.)*

pretty joli(e)

price prix *(m.)*

problem problème *(m.)*

programmer programmeur (-euse)

protect protéger

punish punir

put (on) mettre

quarter quart *(m.)*

question question *(f.)*; **out of the question** pas question

quickly vite, rapidement

rain pleuvoir; pluie *(f.)*

raincoat imperméable *(m.)*

read lire

reasonable raisonnable

receive recevoir

recipe recette *(f.)*
red rouge
refrigerator réfrigérateur *(m.)*
remain rester
repair réparer
repeat répéter
respond répondre
responsible responsable
restaurant restaurant *(m.)*
return *(home)* rentrer; **return** *(an item)* rendre, retourner
rich riche
river fleuve *(m.)*
road route *(f.)*, chemin *(m.)*
roof toit *(m.)*
room chambre *(f.)*
ruler règle *(f.)*

sad triste
salad salade *(f.)*
same même
sandal sandale *(f.)*
say dire
school école *(f.)*
sea mer *(f.)*
see voir
seize saisir
selfish égoïste
sell vendre
send envoyer
sentence phrase *(f.)*
set: set the table mettre le couvert
share partager
shirt chemise *(f.)*
shoes chaussures *(f. pl.)*
shop faire les courses
short court(e)
shorts shorts *(m. pl.)*
show montrer
shy timide
sick malade
sing chanter
sister sœur *(f.)*
skate patin; patiner; **to go ice skating** faire du patin à glace

ski ski *(m.)*; **go skiing** faire du ski; **ski instructor** moniteur de ski *(m.)*
skirt jupe *(f.)*
sky ciel *(m.)*
slacks pantalon *(m.)*
sleep dormir
sleep sommeil *(m.)*; **to be sleepy** avoir sommeil
slowly lentement
small petit(e)
sneaker basket *(f.)*; tennis *(f.)*
snow neiger; neige *(f.)*
so donc; si
soccer football *(m.)*
sock chaussette *(f.)*
soft doux *(f. douce)*
some du, de la, de l', des, en
sometimes quelquefois, parfois
son fils *(m.)*
song chanson *(f.)*
soup soupe *(f.)*
south sud *(m.)*, midi *(m.)*
souvenir souvenir *(m.)*
Spanish espagnol
speak parler
spend dépenser *(money)*; passer *(time)*
sport sport *(m.)*
spring printemps *(m.)*
stamp timbre *(m.)*
start commencer (à); **start out** se mettre en route
station gare *(f.)*
stay rester
stereo chaîne stéréo *(f.)*
store magasin *(m.)*
story histoire *(f.)*
street rue *(f.)*
strict sévère
strong fort(e)
student élève *(m. / f.)*, étudiant(e)
study étudier
subway métro *(m.)*
succeed réussir

success succès *(m.)*
sugar sucre *(m.)*
suitcase valise *(f.)*
summer été *(m.)*
sun soleil *(m.)*; **to be sunny** faire du soleil
sweater pull *(m.)*
swim nager
swim suit maillot de bain *(m.)*
swimming nage, natation *(f.)*; **swimming pool** piscine *(f.)*

table table *(f.)*; **set the table** mettre le couvert
take prendre; apporter; **take a trip** faire un voyage; **take a walk** faire une promenade, se promener; **take care of** garder
tall grand(e)
taste goûter
teacher professeur *(m.)*, maître *(m.)*
telephone téléphone *(m.)*; **on the telephone** au téléphone; **telephone book** annuaire; **telephone booth** cabine *(f.)*
television télévision *(f.)*
tell dire
terrace terrasse *(f.)*
than que
thank you merci
that que; qui; ce, cet, cette
theater théâtre *(m.)*
then puis, alors, ensuite
there là; y; **over there** là-bas; **there is / are** il y a; voilà
these ces
thing chose *(f.)*
think penser
thirst soif *(f.)*; **to be thirsty** avoir soif
this ce, cet, cette
this is voici
those ces
thousand mille, mil *(in dates)*

tidy ranger
tie cravate *(f.)*
time temps *(m.)*; **all the time** tout le temps; **from time to time** de temps en temps; **have a good time** s'amuser; **a long time** longtemps; **on time** à l'heure
to à; **in order to** pour
today aujourd'hui
together ensemble
toilet toilettes *(f. pl.)*
tomorrow demain *(m.)*
too aussi
tooth dent *(f.)*
tourist touriste *(m. / f.)*
towards vers
tower tour *(f.)*
town ville *(f.)*
toy jouet *(m.)*
train train *(m.)*; **by train** en train; **train station** gare *(f.)*
travel voyager
tree arbre *(m.)*
trip voyage *(m.)*; **to take a trip** faire un voyage
true vrai(e)
truth vérité *(f.)*
try essayer (de)

United States États-Unis *(m. pl.)*
umbrella parapluie *(m.)*
under sous
undress se déshabiller
unhappy triste, malheureux
university université *(f.)*
upstairs en haut; **go upstairs** monter

useful utile
useless inutile
usually généralement, d'habitude

vacation vacances *(f. pl.)*; **to go on vacation** aller en vacances
vacuum aspirateur *(m.)*; **to vacuum** passer l'aspirateur
vegetable légume *(m.)*
very très
visit visiter

wait (for) attendre
waitress serveuse *(f.)*
wake réveiller; **wake (oneself)** se réveiller
walk marcher; promener; **to go for a walk** se promener; **to take a walk** se promener
walkman baladeur *(m.)*
wall mur *(m.)*
want désirer, vouloir
wash laver; **wash (oneself)** se laver
watch regarder
watch montre *(f.)*
water eau *(f.)*; **mineral water** eau minérale
weak faible
wear porter
weather temps *(m.)*
week semaine *(f.)*
weekend fin *(f.)* de semaine
well bien

west ouest *(m.)*
what que, qu'est-ce que, quoi; quel(le); ce que
when quand
where où
white blanc *(f.* blanche)
who qui
whole entier (-ière); tout
whom qui
why pourquoi
wife femme *(f.)*
win gagner
wind vent *(m.)*; **to be windy** faire du vent
wine vin *(m.)*
winter hiver *(m.)*; **winter sports** *(m. pl.)* sports d'hiver
wise sage
with avec
without sans
woman femme *(f.)*
wonderful merveilleux (-euse), formidable
word mot *(m.)*
work travailler; marcher *(machines)*; travail *(m.)*
world monde *(m.)*
write écrire

year an *(m.)*; **to be . . . years old** avoir... ans
yes oui
yesterday hier
yet encore; **not yet** pas encore
young jeune; **young people** jeunes gens *(m. pl.)*